Quotes from the Lakeside

collected by

Howard Johnson

includes

Many Favorite Quotes, Letters, Essays, Commentary, and Poetry

Many of the Quotes, and Poems are from other authors

Copyright © 2013 by Howard Johnson.

ISBN: 978-0-9913838-9-4

All rights reserved. No part of this book may be reproduced or transmitted in any form or by any means, electronic or mechanical, including photocopying, recording, or by any information storage and retrieval system, without permission in writing from the copyright owner.

This book was printed in the United States of America.

This book is available at special discounts for bulk purchases for sales promotions, premiums, fund raising, or educational use. For details, contact:

Special Sales - Senesis Word

FAX: - 904-825-0222

Website: www.Ho2Jo.com

Email: senesisword@yahoo.com

QLSQuo_txt17707W

The cover:

   Our home on Lake Tippecanoe in Northern Indiana greets a bright, warm August afternoon in 2003. This photo was taken from a boat immediately in front of our place. This property was a wooded swamp when my father purchased it in 1955. The swamp was filled in 1957 and the home was built and my folks moved into it in 1958. It became a marvelous gathering place for family and friends for many years. They both enjoyed it from then until 1971, the last summer they were both there. My dad died early in 1972. After that, my mom spent a number of summers there with a stream of visits from family and friends. I spent several wonderful summers with her, reprises of summers we spent together at the old cottage around the point which I had purchased from them. In my books of memoirs, there are numerous stories of Mom and me and other family members during many wonderful summers there and at our other lake homes.

   Because of this and because I spent a total of 83 summers at Tippy, 25 of them living full time in this house, it is a very important part of who I am. It was home to my late wife, Barbara, and me for 13 years. Like my parents before us, we had many family reunions up through 2012 and visits from many friends.

   When I was a boy there were many times I played alone and with friends in the wooded swamp that covered the property. We hunted frogs, turtles, snakes and salamanders on the shore and in the swamp. By August the swamp dried up and we could walk freely through the area. We built hide-a-ways under the upturned roots of fallen trees. I tell stories about many of the trees in the back yard, trees I remember from my childhood.

DEDICATION

This book is a lot of who I am, what I think, what I believe, what I imagine, what I dream of, why and whom I love . . . in short, it is a collection of bits and pieces of me as expressed in thoughts and ideas of many people. I collected these words and wrote some over many years of my life. These are also included in my two books of memoirs, *Words from the Lakeside* and *Memoirs from the Lakeside*. These words bring to mind many of those beautiful human beings who, through love and some blunt trauma, helped me become the person I am. Therefore, I dedicate this book with great love and affection to all of my family, friends, and others, whose actions helped create, guide, inspire, stimulate, and mold my life into the person I am today. My passionate desire to please and never to displease them has guided me in positive directions throughout my lifetime. The family members, lovers, friends, mentors, and teachers who have left this earth are remembered fondly, appreciated greatly, and sorely missed. I am powerfully blessed to have known all of these incredible people, family, friends, colleagues, and acquaintances.

I have decided to list in this dedication as many of those people as I can without creating an entire new book. They are remembered in roughly chronological order. Many of these important people have roles in stories and essays inmy memoirs books. I have been blessed with a close, loving relationship with members of my family, unique to each one. Those described as *special* were not loved any more than others. There was something different, maybe *magic*, about the two of us together. It defies definition. There were those, other than family, with which I felt a special connection as well. In my memoir books there is a description of a conversation with one of my grandparents that clearly illustrates my meaning. Those that are not listed are no less loved or appreciated. If I listed all of them, there would be no pages left for the burgeoning content already in place.

The first was of course, my mother, **Ethel Johnson**. A tiny woman, she was still a powerful and loving presence to all who knew her. Mom was a dedicated Christian with all of the best that can mean. She was a loving mother, in the best sense of that calling. She was also a shining example of a truly decent person to everyone she met for the entire 96 years she was alive on this planet. To my knowledge, every organization she joined in her life elected her president. She was loved by all family and friends who knew her.

My father, **Howard R. Johnson**, was a decent, honorable, Christian man. He was as terrific and faithful a father as a boy, then a young man could have. Our close, extended relationship continued when we were in business together for nearly twenty years. A stable, dependable man, he taught me that tears were a manly expression saying only brave and secure men cry openly. Many of the most joyous moments in my life were when I made him proud of me. I will never forget the countless happy hours we spent together, or the experiences we shared.

My grandparents, **Eva May** and **George Dickinson**, were the only grandparents I knew. My father's parents both died before I was old enough to remember. *Grandma Dick* was a strong and loving woman who taught me a great deal. *Granddad Dick* and I had a special, close relationship that was reinforced during numerous fishing trips. Granddad Dick was a master story teller and wove his magic on me frequently, when I was quite young. He taught me much about the realities of life, and how to deal with them.

Many a time when one of his stories was being woven on their porch I would hear Grandma Dick calling from elsewhere in the house, "George! You quit filling that boy's head with your nonsense."

Granddad would grow silent for a moment then resume with a much softer voice.

My sisters, one a virtual second mother, the other, my nemesis during my childhood, added their individual, loving touches to whom I am. Both, like our mother and father, were deeply Christian women, but quite different in their passions and how they practiced their religion. **Lois**, twelve years my senior was much like our father, even being born on his birthday. A strong willed yet gentle and loving force, she and I were extremely close. **Roberta** or **Bobbie**, six years older than I, had a temperament different from Lois's. We fought constantly when we were young, typical sibling battles, but often quite passionate. As adults we still battle occasionally over differences of opinions, but those differences have no effect on the strong bonds, of love and respect, we have for each other.

My two brothers-in-law, Lois's husband **Harold**, and Bobbie's **Robert** were as fine a set of brothers as a man could have. As different as my two sisters, they were a positive influence on others and especially on their *little brother* or *Bro*.

There were aunts, uncles, and cousins, who brought joy and companionship to early days. Though most are now passed away, they are all remembered fondly. Of those few remaining, several are still kept in contact if only with Christmas cards.

DEDICATION

There are nephews and nieces and their families in almost countless numbers, the next generation now carrying the torch of family. They are also loved and treasured. There are many among the group with whom I have a special relationship. You know who you are and what I mean.

The *lovers* in my life have had a staggering emotional impact on the person I am. There are stories about most of them herein. I will not provide the details, some of which could be painful to many people involved. Needless to say, each of them was loved deeply and passionately. I still care deeply for each of them and know the love shared with each diminishes in no way the love for any of the others.

Dolores was my first love, professed at 17, who became my wife and the mother of five of my children. A dedicated and devoted mother, she sacrificed many times for our children. After many happy years with our large brood, our marriage fell apart, and we were divorced. With the well being of our children foremost in each of our minds, we kept our difficulties hidden as best we could. Neither of us ever said a bad or harmful thing about the other to any of our brood. Time softened our feelings and buried our differences. We enjoyed a friendly relationship until her death.

Caroline rescued me from the depths of depression and helped me regain my lost self esteem. Her love and compassion were the most powerful forces in turning my life from the angry, damaging path I had chosen. She presented me with a beautiful daughter in 1968. For several reasons and in spite of our great affection for each other, we parted company when Kristen was three. To my boundless joy, we have been reconciled and are now friends.

Iola came into my life a few years after I left Cleveland and moved to Chicago to try to put my life back in some kind of order. Once more I stumbled into a truly exceptional woman who helped me restore my devastated self respect. Iola has two delightful daughters who became, and remain to this day, as two of my own. After a number of years together, we drifted apart when I moved to Indiana.

Barbara, my wife and companion for the *golden* years, brought joy and her two delightful grown sons into our marriage. She also filled my life with love and spirited activity. When I began writing seriously, she became my editor and critic. She was positively brutal with a red pen. Her efforts contributed a great deal directly to this book.

After we were married, she became a Methodist pastor and led a small country congregation in a church "in the middle of three cornfields" as she always said.

A committed Christian, she took to the ministry with a vigor and determination that grew the small church considerably. With both of us far from any family, the congregation became our family, *warts and all* as she frequently remarked. I was so proud of her accomplishments in the pulpit and with the many members who loved her dearly and showed it. It was devastating to us both when she had to step down because of failing health. The outpouring of accolades and tears from the congregation on her last day in the pulpit was overwhelming. She left us at far too early an age and is now missed terribly, and will continue to be.

Daphne, who came into my life possibly through the efforts of my guardian angel, is now my passion, my lover, and my dearest friend. It is our sincere hope we can enjoy many of the *golden years* together and then go peacefully. She brought her large family into my life as well as her circle of friends. With four daughters, two sons, and thirteen grandchildren, they are an impressive group. I feel a special bond with her children and their spouses who have each treated me with grace and warm affection. Those of her grandchildren I have had the opportunity to get to know have treated me in the same gracious manner. Each is now a vital part of my life. Her many friends have become my friends as well.

My children and grandchildren are a precious legacy of deep and everlasting love. Again, there is much about each of them in my memoirs. I am so proud of what they have accomplished, and the individuals they have become.

Deborah, **Debby**, or **Deb**, is a delightful and energetic woman, the mother of two grown sons and grandmother of my first great-grandchild, Kelan. A dedicate career educator, she is a hard worker, leader, and friend to others. The winter I spent with her after losing Barb was a precious time of remembering, healing, and getting on with my life. It was a joyful, lifting experience at a time when I needed to be lifted.

Howard Michael, **Mike**, or **Noward** to his siblings, is the kind of son many men dream of having. He has three accomplished sons of his own. The oldest, Russ, and his wife presented me with my second great grand child, a girl named Jameson.

Roberta, **Robbie**, **Rob** is a full-time mother to three teenage girls. The quiet one of her siblings, she is a softly loving woman with deep emotions.

DEDICATION

Diana, or **Dee Dee** is a vivacious bundle of energy and love. The *Aunty Mame* of our family, there is never a dull moment when she is around.

Melinda, or **Mindy**, is the delightful, loving mother to an active young son and a daughter who is a dynamo of loving energy. We have a particularly close and uniquely loving relationship.

Kristen, Caroline's daughter, came back into my life in the summer of 2009 after a long absence to my utter amazement, boundless joy, and incomparable loving delight. Mother of two adorable little girls I met for the first time a few months later, she, her husband Vince, and those two little girls have fulfilled my long-held fond dreams of reunion with buckets of tears of sheer joy.

To the various spouses and children of my children I am especially indebted and enamored. I could write pages about each of you and your spouses or *significant others*, but this would then take several volumes. Let it be known you are all treasures of my heart and enjoyable to be with. Sadly, our times shared together are far too few.

To the many friends I have enjoyed during each of the passages of my life I say, thanks for the memories. Though many of you from the early years have lost touch, I remember you fondly. I especially treasure the memories and renewed contact enjoyed at our fiftieth Heights High reunion in 1996 and the sixty-fourth in 2011. There are many friends from the forty-five years of membership in the Euclid Avenue Christian Church now in Cleveland Heights, Ohio. Then there are the new friends brought into my life by moves and relationships. My membership in the Leesburg United Methodist Church brought new friends. My marriage to Barbara and the church she served, Morris Chapel United Methodist Church, brought more new and dear friends. Many of those I mentioned are close and cherished to this day.

Since the latest passage of my life has taken me to St. Augustine, I have garnered many new and close friends. I have become a member of two singing groups here, Singers by the Sea, and the St Augustine Community Chorus. These and the Socrates discussion group I joined have each brought new friendships. I am actively involved in The Florida Writers Association as well as several critique groups of writers. I am a participant in a group of talented writers who meet and share memoirs and short stories each week at the Council on aging. I am pursuing my thespian activities in a drama group, The Riverhouse Players, at the Council on Aging. Also, I give lectures on several subjects including energy and global warming. These are all important new parts of my life.

I close this dedication with a repeat of the true words with which I started.

This book is a lot of who I am, what I think, what I believe, what I imagine, what I dream of, why and whom I love . . . in short, it is a collection of bits and pieces of me as expressed in thoughts and ideas of many people. I collected these words and wrote some over many years of my life. These are also included in my two books of memoirs, **Words from the Lakeside** *and* **Memoirs from the Lakeside**. *These words bring to mind many of those beautiful human beings who, through love and some blunt trauma, helped me become the person I am. Therefore, I dedicate this book with great love and affection to all of my family, friends, and others, whose actions helped create, guide, inspire, stimulate, and mold my life into the person I am today. My passionate desire to please and never to displease them has guided me in positive directions throughout my lifetime. The family members, lovers, friends, mentors, and teachers who have left this earth are remembered fondly, appreciated greatly, and sorely missed. I am powerfully blessed to have known all of these incredible people, family, friends, colleagues, and acquaintances.*

Contents

Dedication.. i
Contents... vii
Preface.. xviii
Why I Write... xxiv
ACKNOWLEDGEMENTS... 141

Works of the following authors are found scattered throughout the book. These include numerous quotes of unknown authors plus many of my own sayings.

Index of Quoted authors - alphabetical by last name:

                                                                            Page

Peter Abelard.. 79
John Emrich Eward Dalberg Acton.. 60
John Adams... 95, 135
Alfred Adler... 30
Fred Allen... 125
Woody Allen.. 124
Mario Andretti.. 115
Maya Angelou... 117
Antoine de Saint Exupéry... 93, 114
Deborah Archer... 61
Aristotle... 27, 99, 116-118, 121, 123
Isaac Asimov.. 113
Saint Augustine... -v-, 39, 120
Richard Bach.. 120
Honore de Balzac... 121
Henry Ward Beecher.. 39
Cyrano de Bergerac... 34
Ingrid Bergman... 122
Yogi Berra... 12, 20, 120
Ambrose Bierce... 112, 116, 122, 131
Smiley Blanton.. 28, 29, 96
William J. H. Boetcker.. 56
Niels Bohr... 118
Charlotte Bronte.. 28

Mel Brooks. 119
Elizabeth Barrett Browning. 99, 100
Robert Browning.. 99
William Jennings Bryan. 83
Art Buchwald. 132
Edward George Bulwer-Lytton... 107
Bumper Sticker. 116
Luther Burbank... 124
G. B. Burgin. 114
Edmond Burke. 128
George Burns... 108
James Branch Cabell. 17
Al Capone... .... 59, 122
George Washington Carver... 75
Douglas Casey... 95
Cato the Elder... 129
Katherine Cebrian. 121
Charlie Chaplin... 119
Gilbert Keith Chesterton. 79, 86, 111
Chief Joseph, Nez Perce. 101
Chinese Proverb. 80
Sir Winston Churchill... .... 3, 17, 107, 112, 118, 127, 128, 132, 134
Cicero. 17, 59, 115
Tom Clancy.. 12
Von Clausewit... 131
Samuel Clemmons (Mark Twain)
    .... -xxiii-, 13, 17, 86, 97, 122, 124, 125, 129, 132, 134
Irvin S. Cobb... 132
Jean Cocteau. 115
Samuel Taylor Coleridge... .... -xxiv-
Confucius. 3, 87
William Congreve... 127
Orin L. Crain. 79
Dr. Frank Crane. 136
Seymour Cray (super computer guy). 132

Contents

e. e. cummings	101
Salvidor Dali	120
Clarence Darrow	114
Guy Davenport	117
Sir Humphrey Davy	90
Richard Dawkins	39
Howard Dean	16
Rene Descartes	102
Philip K. Dick	89
Charles Dickens	131
Edgar Dijkstra	108
Paul Dirac	118
Walt Disney	120
Henry Austin Dobson	46
Will Allen Dromgoole	85
Peter F. Drucker	134
Duchess of Windsor	121
Charles H. Duell	129
Will Durant	114
Jimmy Durante	111
Abba Eban	125, 126
Meister Eckhart	136
Umberto Eco	111
Thomas Alva Edison	24, 133
Albert Einstein	30, 39-42, 111, 114, 117-119, 133, 134
T. S. Eliot	95, 126
Scott Elledge	123
George Elliott	29, 112
Ralph Waldo Emerson	70, 122
Epictetus	6, 17, 76, 123, 134
Paul Erdos	106
Etheridge	28, 29
Oriana Fallaci	105
Richard J. Ferris	124
Williston Fish	13, 14

Ian Fleming.	112, 121
Henry Ford.	102
Benjamin Franklin.	20, 127, 129
Milton Friedman.	54
Robert Frost.	115
Buckminster Fuller.	118
Tony Galento.	101
Galileo Galilei.	31
Mahatma Gandhi.	114 116, 128
Charles de Gaulle.	119, 121
Carl Friedrich Gauss.	128
J. Paul Getty.	112
Albert Giacometti (sculptor).	113
Rosie Giesie.	119
Gail Godwin.	120
Johann Wolfgang von Goethe.	6, 31, 117, 120, 126
Auric Goldfinger (by Ian Flemmimg).	121
Bruce Gould.	135
Zane Grey.	82
David L. Griffith.	139
Ernesto Che Guevara.	127
Sacha Guitry.	121
Moses Hadas.	30, 122
Lucille S. Harper.	120
Robert Heinlein.	26, 69
Ernest Hemingway.	17, 123, 126
Jimi Hendrix.	114
Oliver Herford.	122
Charleton Heston.	24
Gertrude Himmelfarb.	83
Bill Hirst.	119
Adolph Hitler.	59
C. A. R. Hoare.	119
Eric Hoffer.	-xi-, 31, 64, 83, 87, 89, 95
William M. Holden.	127

Contents

Oliver Wendell Holmes	130
Sherlock Holmes	112
Mary Howitt	86
Elbert Hubbard	113
Charles Evans Hughes	82
Sigfried Hulzer	127
Aldous Huxley	112
Thomas Henry Huxley	108
Robert G. Ingersoll	79
Helen Hunt Jackson	77
Thomas Jefferson	6, 17, 25, 46, 102, 133
Howard R. Johnson	35
Thomas Jones	122
Erica Jong	116, 117
Nora Joyce (wife of James)	126
Carl Gustav Jung	115
Alan Kay	127
John Keats	29, 99
John F. Kennedy	30, 96, 101, 112
Robert Kennedy	96
Jason Kidd	20
Soren Aabye Kierkegaard	6, 9, 39
Herb Kimmel	123
Martin Luther King Jr.	102, 108
Rudyard Kipling	91, 131
Henry Kissinger	114, 120
Irving Kristol	130
Gloria Leonard	56, 123
Leviticus, Chapter 19:16 NIV	89
George Lichtenberg	116
A. J. Liebling	39
Abraham Lincoln	115, 129, 133
Henry Wadsworth Longfellow	93
Alice Roosevelt Longworth	111
How Chee Loo	101

Father Larry Lorenzoni 127
Samuel Lover 74
Douglas MacArthur 132
Ross MacDonald 124
Niccolo Machiavelli 20
Norman Mailer 95
Mark Twain (Samuel Clemmons)
. . . . -xxiii-, 13, 17, 86, 97, 122, 124, 125, 129, 132, 133
Andrew Marvell 106
Groucho Marx 113
Karl Marx . . . . 89 , 94, 134
Juan Matus 33
Cormac McCarthy 33
Pearl Yeadon McGinnis 89
Golda Meir 26
Henry Louis Mencken 124, 126, 131
Bob Metcalfe 118
Wilson Mizner 125
Angela Monet . . . . -xxii-, 8, 115
Marilyn Monroe 134
Wiliam Vaughn Moody 137
Saint Thomas More 26
Talbot Mundy 12, 18, 31, 59, 60, 65, 78, 79, 81, 83, 86, 97, 100
H. H. Munro 108, 119
Napoleon Bonaparte 107, 108
John von Neumann 118
Joseph Forte Newton 100
Friedrich Nietzsche 106-108, 114, 123, 132
Aaron Nimzovich 124
Anias Nin 26
Dorothy Law Nolte 54, 130
Sterling North 83
Laura Nyro 90
Barack Hussein Obama 31, 59, 60, 82, 88, 90
Flannery O'Connor 20, 115

Contents

Ken Olson	131
Aristotle Onassis	117, 121
Robert J. Oppenheimer	122
Robert Orben	125
George Orwell	76, 84, 94
Samuel Palmer	117
George S. Patton	31, 121, 129
Wolfgang Pauli	132
Lucius Aemilius Paullus	94
Randy Pausch	113
Lewis Perelman	127
Wilfred A. Peterson	80
Pablo Picasso	108
Timothy Pickering	133
Robert Pirsig	38
Plato	27, 101, 102, 106, 110, 117, 123, 130
J. R. Pope	87
W. B. Prescott	118
Henning Webb Prentis, Jr.	57
Elvis Presley	115
Don Quixote (author Cervantes)	112
Ayn Rand	10, 13, 24, 108
Branch Rickey	1201
James Whitcomb Riley (The Hoosier poet)	138
Harold Robbins	123
Sir Stephen Henry Roberts	126
Francois de La Rochefoucauld	135
Johns D. Rockefeller	90
Will Rogers	128, 129, 131
Theodore (Teddy) Roosevelt	134
Gioacchino Rossini	82
Helen Rowland	127, 135
Bertrand Russell	117, 119, 128
Sadi	116
Sagan	113

Saint Albertus Magnus.	33
Saint Augustine (354-430).	39, 120
Saint Francis of Assisi.	1
Saint Teresa of Avila.	86
Saint Thomas More (1478-1535).	26
Sanscrit.	3, 34
George Santayana.	125
Jean-Paul Sartre.	83, 111, 122
Courtland Sayers.	76
Anne Wilson Schaef.	89
Friedrich von Schiller.	111
Arthur Schopenhauer.	113
Charles M. Schulz (Cartoonist - Peanuts).	128
Arnold Schwarzenegger.	106
Albert Schweitzer.	90
Sir Walter Scott.	87
Seneca (3BC - 65AD).	116
George Bernard Shaw.	95, 96, 111, 115, 117, 121, 123, 127
Brenda Shears.	80
Edward Rowland Sill.	135
Charles Simmons.	134
Simonides.	115
Gary Allen Sledge.	135
Fred Smith.	55, 130
Socrates.	98, 102, 116, 134
Thomas Sowell.	78, 79
Joseph Stalin.	59, 60
Gloria Steinem.	80
George Stephanopolous.	20
James Stephens.	17
Adlai Stevenson.	126
Robert Louis Stevenson.	71, 94
Tom Stoppard.	126
John Stossel.	55, 56
Igor Stravinsky.	35

Contents

Bjarne Stroustrup... 108
Charles William Stubbs... 125
Savielly Grigorievitch Tartakower... 13
Jeremy Taylor.. 78
Margaret Thatcher... 79
Henry David Thoreau................................. 78, 89, 116, 122, 124, 127
Thumper in "Bambi".. 76
Leo Tolstoy.. 123
Leon Trotsky.. 31
Martin Fraquhar Tupper.. 61
Alexander Tytler or Tyler... 57
Lao-Tzu.. 126
Sun-Tzu.. 126
Paul Valery.. 132
Sheldon Vanauken.. 80
Henry Van Dyke... 137
Balint Vazsonyi... 85
Gore Vidal.. 117, 124
Pancho Villa... 130
Karl Wallenda.. 126
H. M. Warner... 131
George Washington.. 10, 38, 115
Thomas Watson.. 128
H. G. Wells... 107, 108
Mae West... 35, 120
Oscar Wilde........................... 87, 92, 98, 107, 111, 120, 121, 133
Robin Williams... 132
Ludwig Wittgenstein.. 107
Frank Lloyd Wright.. 107, 111
Steven Wright... 112, 121
Bill Wulf... 20
Yoda, from "The Empire Strikes Back"....................................... 102
Frank Zappa.. 113
Zig Ziglar... 134
Emile Zola.. 29

Miscellaneous Commentary, Letters, Essays, and Poetry, Mostly my Own Writing - other authors noted

Preface.	-xviii-
Here are a few comments about my use of the word, "God.".	-xviii-
A collection of my current guiding beliefs and principals.	xix
My measure of a man or woman.	xxii
Why I Write.	xxiv
Truth and Belief.	2
To All My dearly Beloved Children.	2
He Who Knows Not - *unknown*.	3
Sound Rainbow.	4
Flaglar 1037.	5
Comet Hale-Bopp.	6
A Parent's Prayer.	7
Homework, Sports, and Other Educational Problems.	8
A Christmas Gift.	10
Letter to My Grandson on Graduation from High School.	11
The Most Beautiful Will ever Written - *Williston Fish*.	13
Significant Quotes of *Talbot Mundy*.	18
Notable Quotes from the NIV Bible.	21
Notable Quotes from the KJV Bible.	23
Here are a few suggestions for a more pleasant and enjoyable life..	25
What is Love and What Is it About..	26
Greek Words for Love.	27
Poems of and about Love.	28
How Long our Love Will Last - *George Etheridge*.	28
Love me not for Comely Grace - *George Etheridge*.	29
Oh, The Comfort - *George Elliott*.	29
Someone Who Understands - *Smiley Blanton*.	29
LOVE - IMPRESSIONS.	30
Remembering Easter Sunday, 1934 - *66 years ago today*.	32
The Melancholy Days - *Howard R. Johnson*.	35
Writers and Women.	36
Perception.	38
On Prayer *(From the Sermon on the Mount)*.	39
Relativity and a Totally New Concept of Our Universe.	40
Sailing With the Lake Tippecanoe Sailing Club.	47
If a Child Lives with - - - *Dorothy Law Nolte*.	54

Contents

From Consumer Advocate, *Johns Stossel* 55
Enigma - *Deborah Horlak* 61
Epilog to Enigma 61
Reflections on and about Columbus Day 62
The Calling 66
Images of Pain 75
One Midnight Deep in Starlight Still - *Courtland Sayers* 76
October's Bright Blue Weather - *Helen Hunt Jackson* 77
Slow Me Down, Lord - *Orin L. Crain* 79
Heroes and Oracles 81
On Idealism 81
What any Man Can Do - *Zane Gray* 82
One Man's Opinion On Being a Christian 84
The Bridge Builder - *Will Allen Dromgoole* 85
Beauty of Face 87
Another New Serenity Prayer 87
To Reach Another Mind and Heart 88
The Past is that Portion of Time 89
IF - *Rudyard Kipling* 91
It Is Not Easy - *unknown* 92
When Things go Wrong - *unknown* 93
Come With Me to Macedonia and Fight - *Lucius Aemilius Paullus* 94
Ineptocracy - *unknown* 95
One Valuable ThingI Learned About Children 96
As you think, you travel 97
Good and Evil, Right and Wrong 98
How do I Love Thee - *Elisabeth Barrett Browning* 100
To Do Is to Live 102
Two Wolves - *Cherokee tale* 103
To My Dearly Beloved Grandchildren 104
Love Them and Let Them Be 106
Dream Thoughts 109
Midnight - Morning - Haiku 129
If a Person Lives With Criticism - *Dorothy Law Nolte, rewritten* 130
John Adams, 1812 letter to Timothy Pickering, *Pub 1850* 133
The Golden Rule 135
Pandora's Song - *Willliam Vaughn Moody* 137
When the Frost is on the Punkin - *James Whitcomb Riley* 138
Too Soon Old - (Crabby Old Man) - *Dave Griffith* 139
ACKNOWLEDGMENTS 141

PREFACE

Over the years, I have collected, written, and saved many stories, quotes, comments, letters, and poems. These include facts, ideas, thoughts, hypotheses, or theories from my mind and soul. There are about 500 of these from at least 270 different individuals including myself. My purpose in collecting these quotes and in putting them in this book is to share these with others. I designed it to be a book one can pick up and read for a few minutes or for hours. Its content runs from single lines to multi-page stories, memoirs from my life. My own opinions on numerous subjects are sprinkled liberally throughout the book. Like every other human mind, I may be right or wrong. I try to think and also to write in a rational way, rather than emotional, especially about those subjects that require or could use serious, thoughtful effort. It is quite difficult to keep those emotions from breaking into even serious, rational discourse, but at least I make the effort. Things of the heart and soul, however, are tied much more to feelings and emotions. I hope the reader will feel my emotions as they have a powerful effect on this work in virtually every part of life where feelings participate.

Much of the first section of this book describes concepts that make sense to me and feelings I have personally experienced. I believe one's personal belief system will determine one's social, religious, and political beliefs; their relationships with others; the kind of life they lead; and ultimately, the person they are at any given time. There are numerous pieces about my personal belief systems. They describe the most significant of my guiding principles. Some describe how I try to relate to my children, a most salient part of who I am.

Here are a few comments about my use of the word, "God."

"God" has been used by man for ages as the name or explanation for everything inexplicable—the unknown—the mysteries—the unfathomable. It is not a meaningless or empty term no matter what your belief system. Simply stated. "God" is a term that means and is interchangeable with "the order of things" or "natural law" or even "the inexplicable." Many anthropomorphize it to mean, "The man up in heaven." When

PREFACE

fundamentalist atheists say, "there is no God," they are actually declaring their personal distaste for what the term implies religiously—the anthropomorphic father figure. As with many terms, individuals will attach their own meaning to "God." If you are one of those offended by or prejudiced against the term for any reason, simply substitute mentally "the order of things," or any other term that fits when you come across the word, "God" in my writing. I'm sure there are other words that could be considered offensive to some readers for we all have our own abhorrence to different things, words included. Should you come across any of these, simply substitute mentally a less offensive word or phrase. As some wise person once said, "Blessed are the flexible for they shall not be bent out of shape."

The following statements are a collection of my current basic beliefs relating to interactions with other individuals. I provide it so you can better understand the basis and origin of what I have to say. It explains how I see myself and how to understand my words. I call it my Survival Guide for Senior Years:

I am a believer in myself and those individuals I trust.

I trust no politician, political operative, political activist, government official, celebrity, elitist intellectual, or media reporter or talking head I do not know personally, and few of those I do. I trust no Muslim, ever. Their religious principles make this imperative.

I trust and admire the rational opinions and logical judgements of those looked down on by elitists, the so-called *common people*. Their wisdom is far greater than that for which they are given credit. However, I do not trust their opinions or judgements when based on emotions, because they are often influenced and persuaded by those described in the previous paragraph.

I do not expect anyone to understand any of that which they do not know. I do not even expect them to understand much of what they do know.

I see politics, religion, pseudo science, ethnicity, and culture as powerful belief systems often used by unscrupulous individuals to control others for their own purpose.

I am not a follower of or beholden to any ism, group belief system (religious, political, cultural, or other), political party, union, corporation, peer group, boss or officer (political, union, corporate or other organizational at any level), grant committee, dean or head of faculty, or any similar person or organization. This is why I am free to express my own opinions without disrespect, concern for, or apologies to anyone or any group. I will change my own beliefs to fit new realities and knowledge when and if the new information or understanding requires it.

I consider myself a truly independent and quite liberal individual, a realist who knows what it means to conserve, an equal opportunity supporter or detractor. As such, I know my words and opinions may offend, but it is never my intent to do so. There are exceptions, of course.

I am not ever in any way controlled, intimidated or cowed by any kind of political correctness. I believe it to be a creation of the many narcissist members of the entertainment world and in particular the TV news media. These self-serving hypocrites use PC to coerce people into speaking and thinking the way they determine. It is one more system elitist intellectuals use to try to control others, especially the gullible, unthinking lemmings so many people, including Americans, have become.

I will not accept as a fact, any words, concepts or ideas that do not meet the tests of logic, reason and/or hard science as I understand them. My opinions and beliefs are subject to change when and if new information makes a change necessary. I see the inflexible, closed mind - the mind of the fundamentalist of any flavor: religious, political, social, cultural, or other, right, left, or in the middle - as an evil curse on the individual whose mind is closed for any reason.

I no longer have patience for certain things, mostly personal things, not because I've become arrogant, but simply because I reached a point in my life where I do not want to waste time with what displeases me or hurts me. I lost the will to please those who do not like me, to love those who do not love me, to smile at those who do not want to smile at me, and be around those who cause me pain. I have a strong will to please those who like me, love those who love me, smile at all but those detractors mentioned earlier, and be around those who bring me joy. I no longer spend a single minute on those who lie, fake affection, or want to manipulate. I decided not to coexist anymore with pretense, hypocrisy, dishonesty, political correctness and cheap praise. I have no patience for cynicism, excessive criticism and demands of any nature. However, I do

PREFACE

solicit and encourage constructive criticism of my professional actions, especially my writing. I seek that which will improve and add value to my work

It is clear to me that thousands of free and independent individuals and groups working in a favorable competitive environment, under a capitalist system with limited government in a democratic republic, are infinitely superior in every conceivable way to a central decision making collectivist body or government of any kind. The bigger and more powerful the government, the less freedom individuals have to grow and improve their life and the lower will be the standard of living under such government. Examples of this reality abound now and throughout history for at least the last 3,000 years. Freedom works. Collectivism works solely for those running the system and leads to impoverishment, dependency, and ultimately some form of slavery for the masses.

I believe in treating all individuals with respect and honesty. These both deserve, and I will expect, respect and honesty in return. However, I see no reason to be bound to do the same when faced with disrespect or dishonesty.

I try to deal with each person with consideration in all of these things
—*Howard Johnson - 2012*

"There are many who find a good alibi far more attractive than an achievement. For an achievement does not settle anything permanently. We still have to prove our worth anew each day: we have to prove that we are as good today as we were yesterday. But when we have a valid alibi for not achieving anything we are fixed, so to speak, for life. Moreover, when we have an alibi for not writing a book, painting a picture and so on, we have an alibi for not writing the greatest book and not painting the greatest picture. Small wonder that the effort expended and the punishment endured in obtaining a good alibi often exceed the effort and grief requisite for the attainment of a most marked achievement."

—*Eric Hoffer*

My expressed opinions may or may not be in accord with the thinking of those who read my words. This includes my views on both of the no-nos of human verbal interaction, religion and politics. Because both areas can be emotionally charged and can be quite devoid of rational thoughts, there is an opportunity to offend, bring to anger, and damage feelings. Those from many emotional persuasions will surely find themselves pricked by barbs from many directions.

I have much respect for the knowledge and wisdom found in the words of many human beings. I even include those deemed foolish and unwise by the multitudes, those whom elitists and intellectuals see as far beneath them in intellect, or brainpower. This even applies to those who populate flyover country. Genius or mentally challenged, corporate president or ditch digger, priest or sinner, person of any age, sex, culture, race, wealth or education—each of these and others have their own set of knowledge from which can be gleaned words of wisdom and truth if one listens.

I do not judge the worth of a person by any of these criteria. To do so is among the greatest faults of those who shut off all sources of knowledge and understanding that could be gained from those with whom they do not see eye to eye. It extends to even the lowliest among us. This fault is exhibited by political or religious elitists who refuse to be involved in communications of any kind that does not agree with or conform to their personal belief system. As a result, their inbred concepts shut out more and more good, even profound knowledge because it does not fall within the limitations of their beliefs, or confirm them. This is why *political correctness* is the political equivalent of *fundamentalist beliefs* in the broad field of religion including atheism. All of these are belief systems driven by emotion, and not necessarily based in reality. One man's belief is another man's anathema.

In 1969, I gave a talk on personal communication at the American Dental Trade Association annual meeting in Chicago. The following comment is from that talk. I used one of my own strong beliefs to illustrate the often hidden but immense value of listening to what even the lowliest among us has to say.

"My measure of a man or woman is not how much they agree with me, but rather, how logical and persuasive are their arguments when they disagree. I also consider what kind of emotions play in these arguments. Do they lash out in anger with words of resentment and condemnation, or do they listen and make rational judgements?"

—*Howard Johnson, from a talk on communication in 1969*

In the areas of human thoughts and ideas, I much prefer to choose my own belief systems based on knowledge, experience, and logical thought processes, rather than adopt those of others. This does not mean I shun the wisdom or counsel of others. It means I

PREFACE

accept such only after checking it through my own understanding of how the universe works. That may seem crazy to some. I address the following saying to them:

Those who dance are thought insane by those who can't hear the music.

—Angela Monet

Hopefully, you will hear and enjoy some of the music of my heart, soul, and imagination which have been liberally poured into these pages. There is one other particular quote I find describes quite beautifully how I have tried to approach life, at least for the last fifty years. It has been attributed to a number of people including Alfred D. Souza whose name appears as the author on a cup I have had for some time. Some research I conducted attributes it to Mark Twain who preceded Souza by a hundred years. The cup displays the last four lines of the words as follow:

Work like you don't need the money.

Dance as though no one is watching you.

Love as though you have never been hurt before.

Sing as though no one can hear you.

Live as though heaven is on earth.

Mark Twain (Samuel Clemens)

Why I Write

I am a story teller, both fiction and memoirs: fabricated and remembered. I have six finished books published and several more that will be published this year. At least I am hopeful they will be finished this year. I have five more writing projects in stages from half finished to just started. There are many more in the idea stage. My writing dreams are far too big for me to accomplish in one lifetime. That alone should help keep me young at heart and thirsting for another day, even at my advanced age. Some time back I told a friend I discovered I am a writer, but I didn't say why. Then I read the following words of Samuel Taylor Coleridge:

"Poetry has been to me its own exceeding great reward; it has given me the habit of wishing to discover the good and beautiful in all that meets and surrounds me."

His words prompted thoughts reminding me how impossible it is for me to write all I have to say I would like to write. Each story, thought, idea, or memory I put into words brings forth from the depths of my mind and imagination, more stories, more thoughts, more ideas, and more memories. I am deliciously excited by writing these things. I have difficulty deserting my writing to take the time to do much else. This passion moves me so strongly that at night in bed, I often stay awake, planning how best to word this story, thought or idea.

For many years I read avidly, devouring all kinds of literature. Once I started writing at age seventy, my reading time gave way to writing time. It has been this way ever since. To me, writing is far more rewarding. I would like my words to be read, but my main pleasure lies in the writing. I would write even if I knew no one would ever read my words.

So think about writing. If there is a story, memory, or idea in you, give it the wings of the written word. Who knows how many others you may touch.

—Howard Johnson, 2011

The content of this book is taken from the first section and parts throughout of my book of memoirs, *Memoire from the Lakeside.* These are writings I have collected from both my reading and my writing since 1945. Many of them have been influential in molding me into the person I am today, or possibly reflect ideas, thoughts and opinions already formed and part of who I am.

I am continuing collecting, recording and writing quips, comments, and opinions, so there might even be another such book before I leave this earth. That reminds me of a saying I wrote at least ten years ago. Old writers never die. They just lose their words.

I believe there are no more fitting words with which to begin this work than those of Saint Francis of Assisi. They have been a guiding light for many decent lives and a beacon of peace and love for centuries.

> Lord, make me an instrument of your peace,
> Where there is hatred, let me sow love;
> where there is injury, pardon;
> where there is doubt, faith;
> where there is despair, hope;
> where there is darkness, light;
> where there is sadness, joy;
> O Divine Master, grant that I may not so much
> seek to be consoled as to console;
> to be understood as to understand;
> to be loved as to love.
> For it is in giving that we receive;
> it is in pardoning that we are pardoned;
> and it is in dying that we are born to eternal life.
>
> —*Saint Francis of Assisi*

Truth and Belief

When truth and belief come to conflict,

it is better to change one's belief to fit the truth

than to change the truth to fit one's belief.

Beliefs are the creations of men

while **Truths are the creations of God!**

—Howard Johnson, July 7, 1986

To all my dearly beloved children,

Your kind of father? I think only maybe. I will always try to be the best I can be for you while remaining my own kind of man. As a father, my kind of man will always try to realize his children are not his possessions, but are growing, separate human beings with their own lives to lead. He is, therefore, responsible for doing the best job he can to teach his children how to cope with the world. He does not have the right to impose his own will on them, but must protect them from danger. He must not be a pal, a dictator, a friend, a slave, or a slave-master to his children. Yet as occasions and situations dictate, he must be each of these and still more.

His relationship must be multidirectional and fluid in all respects. As the child grows, he must constantly adjust to the proper degree of control for both the child's education and protection. He must have the strength to let his charges be hurt so they learn some cautions are in order. He must carefully protect and gauge the amount of hurt to be allowed to both the child's age and constitution.

Likewise, in life's decisions he must grant more and more autonomy as the child gains the experience to handle it. He must maintain a benevolent dictatorship until his charges are on their own. Democracy is suitable for a nation or group of adult equals, but it is a disaster in a family of growing children. He must also recognize it is best to loosen the reigns too early than too late since this teaches the child responsibility for his or her actions. Above all, he must know love is not possession, but sharing.

A wise man was asked how to hold love, to which he replied, "Like a small bird in the hand. Hold it too tightly and it dies; hold it too loosely and it flies away."

I know not how you view your father now, but when you are a full person at whatever age, invite me into your life as you would a friend. If it comes to pass in a comfortable and loving fashion, I will have been the father I intended to be.

—*Howard Johnson, 1965*

He who knows not and knows not that he knows not is a fool. Shun him!
He who knows not and knows that he knows not is a child. Teach him!
He who knows, and knows not that he knows is blind. Lead him!
He who knows and knows that he knows is wise. Follow him!

—*Many versions and sources, Persian saying, Sanscrit, Confucius*

A lie gets halfway around the world before the truth has a chance to get its pants on.

—*Sir Winston Churchill (1874-1965)*

Some are born great, some achieve greatness, and some have greatness thrust upon them.

—*William Shakespeare*

Sound Rainbow

Out of the nothing whiteness they explode. Purple-red sounds and fresh green smells—brittle, crackling things, bright crashing pain. The yellow sea rolls quietly against itself, and two green suns light endlessly a bright blue desert.

Somewhere, a quiet, fur-soft sound begins a trip. Small creatures watch and run, stop and listen, in and out, to and fro.

The fur-soft sound becomes an orange din and searches out the creatures for its own concentric pleasures.

Larger creatures now move and see and listen and slither warmly, silently outward.

The orange din invades the separation of the blue desert, and the yellow sea and the creatures follow for their own pleasures.

The orange din grows into a scarlet scream of terror and realization. The creatures flee and stumble and die. The scarlet scream stands alone between gentle rolls of yellow sea and the fierce blue desert sand. And the two green suns make pleasing smells. The scarlet scream deepens to the purple roar of a thousand purple cataracts of a thousand purple rivers rushing ever onward toward unknown whiteness.

The yellow sea stretches forever, guiding and beckoning the purple roar along its helix path both outward and inward.

Enormous creatures now roll slowly onward between the yellow sea and the blue desert and the purple roar.

The creatures' pleasures are infinite. But the whiteness fear is the bitterest and the sweetest of them all. The creatures lurch and throb; the purple roar turns grayish brown and the whiteness fear engulfs completely.

The yellow sea and the blue desert merge. A green fragrance is born. The green fragrance reaches the two green suns.

The creatures pulse and are gone.

All become one—Silence returns,

Whiteness . . .

0.

—Howard Johnson, 1974

Flaglar 1037

My friend, Flaglar 1037, an alien astrophysicist whom I met in February of 1934 through a timeslip he created, says we humans have it all wrong. The speed of light is not constant, but is a function of the total mass of the universe and the inverse of the square of the distance of the point of measurement to the effective center of mass of the universe. Because the mass in the universe is irregularly distributed, the speed varies somewhat randomly as the measurement is taken near massive objects like black holes, for instance. For this reason, light curves through space under the influence of gravity in a similar way as mass moves in curved paths. Like planets under the gravitational control of a star, or a star under gravitational control of a galaxy, light is under gravitational control of the center of mass of the universe.

When energy or matter (energy slowed and thus trapped in closed three-dimensional loops) reaches the edge or surface of the universe, all mass is in one direction. The light would then *orbit* or *fall* back toward the center of mass in exactly the same way any amount of matter would behave. This results in a universe shaped like a slowly pulsing irregular ball. The irregularities in the microwave background radiation could define the surface of such a universe, but only at one point in time.

Since we on Earth are in a relatively fixed position in the universe relative to its center of mass, light speed measurements always give the same results. For this reason, it will take millions of years for the speed of light to change enough so man can detect the change. We can, however, see the effect of changes in light speed every time we view light from a distant object passing close to a massive object or through a gravitational lens.

This means that light coming to us from a distant galaxy, which we assume came in a straight line, may instead have coursed several times or even hundreds of times through the universe. That galaxy appearing to be billions of light years away, could, in fact, be our own galaxy—its light coming back to us by a circuitous, gravity-routed, irregular path. The red shift we see in distant objects is simply light that has come to us from a place where time is moving much slower and so the frequency of the light waves are much wider, redder. This is the *apparent* doppler shift.

It follows that given enough time, every photon of light and every particle of matter in the universe will eventually pass through the event horizon of some black hole. When the last photon and the last bit of matter have disappeared, and the universe consists only of the remaining black holes, what then?

Flaglar also thinks it will be a long time before man will figure this out. He doubts our species will last that long.

—*Howard Johnson, May 15, 1995*

People understand me so poorly that they don't even understand my complaint about them not understanding me.

—*Soren Aabye Kierkegaard (1813-1855)*

When the people fear the government, there is tyranny. When the government fears the people, there is liberty.

—*Thomas Jefferson*

A person hears only what they understand.

—*Johann Wolfgang von Goethe*

There is only one way to happiness and that is to cease worrying about things which are beyond the power of our will.

—*Epictetus*

We are such stuff as dreams are made on; and our little life Is rounded with a sleep.

—*William Shakespeare*

Comet Hale-Bopp

First visible in the early morning sky about 25° above the horizon in the northeast, comet Hale-Bopp may well be the most spectacular comet display since the appearance of Halley's comet in 1910. It is now at its highest point in the evening sky. Hale-Bopp's nucleus is at least three times the size of Halley's and will remain in view to the naked eye until after the first of May. The comet sank to the horizon in the morning sky, disappearing shortly after April 1. During the same period, it rose in the northwestern evening sky, reaching its highest point on April 14. It will remain visible in the evening until after May 1 (1997).

A comet is a fluffy ball of ice and rock, a sort of *dirty snowball*. As the comet nears the sun and comes inside the orbit of Jupiter, radiation from the sun causes the surface to evaporate, creating streams of dust and gas that make up the comet's tails. The curved tail is glowing dust, and the straight tail is ionized gas. The tails may vary in brightness, direction, and color as differences in the solar wind's magnetic field buffet the nucleus. Changes can be dramatic even in periods as short as half an hour.

Comets are visitors from two clouds of objects held in the sun's gravity out beyond the orbit of Pluto. Called the *Kuiper Belt* and the *Oort cloud,* the objects in these areas are mostly ice and range from tiny specks to Pluto and recently discovered bodies like Eris in the Kuiper belt. There may be even bigger bodies in the Oort cloud. a cloud of debris held in the sun's gravity out beyond the planets. Each object follows its own orbit around the sun. Those objects whose orbit brings them inside the orbit of Jupiter react to the sun's radiation and may become visible. When they are discovered, comets are named for their discoverers. Hale-Bopp is one of these, albeit a spectacular one. Comet orbits are sometimes altered by passing near a planet or other large body. Comet Shoemaker-Levy was one of these. It passed close to Jupiter, whose gravity altered its orbit so much that it broke up into a *train* of some thirty large objects which crashed into Jupiter with spectacular results. Like most comets, Shoemaker-Levy was not visible to the unaided eye but was tracked by astronomers with telescopes.

Highly visible comets appear only once every one or two decades, so be sure to view this spectacular display of a solar system visitor whenever possible.

—*Howard Johnson, April 2, 1997*

A Parent's Prayer

Dear Lord make me a good parent! Teach me to be as courteous to my children as I would have them be to me. When I make decisions contrary to their will, let me be reasonable not arrogant, conciliatory not condescending. Forbid that I should ridicule their mistakes or humiliate them when they displease or confuse me. By my own acts of omission and evasion, let me not teach them to mislead and lie. Make me mindful of the value of direction by example and of the hypocrisy of preaching what is not supported by practice.

When they were young, I was mindful that I could not expect from them the judgment of adults. Now that they are adults, let me be mindful that I should not expect from them the judgment of children. Let me also understand that their adult judgments may differ from mine and keep a careful tongue about those differences.

Let me be to my children a pillar of strength rather than a leaning post. Insofar as it is practical, let me help them to point their ambitions high. Let me also applaud their concerns and encourage their self-fulfillment. Let me not rob them of their opportunities for rewards or deprive them of their responsibility to make decisions and accept the consequences.

Do not allow me to become so distracted by externals that I miss the significance of their inner concerns. Teach me to evaluate, but not exaggerate the shock and impact of hair and holler, beads and barbs, scene and obscene, fiction and friction. Let me share their concern for the world that was bequeathed to them—a world of anxiety and confusion, quite different in many ways from the world of my own youth.

Let me be receptive to ideas and responsive to ideals. Help me show through my own life that I value principles more than expediency, courage more than conformity, individual action with responsibility more than dependency, human values more than monetary. Let me also demonstrate that when I *do my own thing*, I am mindful of its effect on others, and that when my children *do their own thing* I do not sit in judgment. Let me enjoy with love those things we have and do together. Let me not disparage or condemn those things we do not do together for any reason.

Help me love them and leave them be. Make me a good parent for these times.

—*Anonymous quote paraphrased by Howard Johnson, December 2000*

※ ※ ※

Homework, Sports, and Other Education Problems

I'm sure there are parents who drive their children to be overachievers in both academics and sports. I'm equally sure there are even more American parents that take only a passing note of how their children are doing academically, usually to gripe at them at grade time. With the increasing emphasis on sports (prestige and entertainment) over academics, it follows that academics will suffer. This is particularly so in some school systems which glorify sports.

I recently read what to me was an extremely biased article on schools that dealt with homework. The thrust of the article and what most people will get from it is that our poor little darlings are overwhelmed with schoolwork and that something ought to be done about it. The article indicated that since 1981, homework has increased from seventeen minutes to nearly half an hour each school night. That totals two hours and sixteen minutes per week! I realize there is a wide variation between schools, but come on! How many hours a week do those same children watch the idiocy on TV? Or how about sports? Sports practice and games certainly take up far more time than any homework.

Read carefully, it points out how harmful, misguided parental demands of their children can be when filtered through our antiquated school systems. Ignoring the emotional thrust of the article and the two inserts, the obvious conclusion is that good parental interest and instruction at an early age make a tremendous difference in academic success later.

Most inequality in education is caused by parents too uneducated or uncaring to teach their children. The title of the insert alone, *Where It's an Unaffordable Luxury*, defines the content and will give many parents and children an excuse to fail to do what will help them most. A better title would be *An Absolute Necessity Being Ignored*. The poor and uneducated are truly the ones most in need of this luxury. There are solutions, but few are willing to pay the price.

Until people who are disadvantaged for any reason realize that it is up to them to correct the situation for themselves, they will continue to propagate the forces that keep them disadvantaged in the first place. No matter how much money or effort others (families, schools, government programs) spend, overcoming the causes of their disadvantaged status remains their own responsibility. Contrast the cultural attitude of many poor recent immigrant families with so many poor American families of many ethnic backgrounds. Many poor immigrant families pull themselves out of poverty in a single generation while so many poor Americans don't. The big difference? Attitude, expectations, and involvement of the family in the education of the young and the high value placed on education, even when they don't know the language! Historically, poor immigrants from Europe and Asia have succeeded in America from their own hard work, self-education, and determination in spite of massive organized discrimination. Our poor cultural communities of all ethnic types will succeed as they follow those examples, or fail as they concentrate on discrimination and government handouts. As long as they concentrate on excuses and supposed discrimination as the reasons for their sorry state, they will remain there.

Success in life is ensured by teaching children to overcome obstacles and thus preparing them to succeed. That includes teaching them to prepare for life as best they can instead of wallowing in self-pity and being entertained. Sure it's easier for some than for others! The playing field is not even and never will be. There will always be Albert Einsteins and Joe Dumbos albeit many more of the latter than the former. In all people, genetic differences will abound. There will be more basketball failures than Michael Jordans. Placing a high value on a good education (from birth onward) will be more important for the less-than-average than for the average and more important for the average than for the gifted. Education starts with the family. If they don't provide a leg up, life will be an uphill struggle!

—*Howard Johnson, January 22, 1999*

The highest and most beautiful things in life are not to be heard about, nor read about, nor seen but, if one will, are to be lived.

—*Soren Aabye Kierkegaard (1813-1855*

We were both in love with him. I fell out of love with him, but he didn't.

—*Zsa Zsa Gabor*

A slender acquaintance with the world must convince every man that actions, not words, are the true criterion of the attachment of friends.

—*George Washington*

It only stands to reason that where there's sacrifice, there's someone collecting the sacrificial offerings. Where there's service, there is someone being served. The man who speaks to you of sacrifice is speaking of slaves and masters, and intends to be the master.

—*Ayn Rand*

A Christmas Gift

I have tried hard to think of a Christmas gift I could send to all of you. This would be an impossibility in itself. Instead I send a wish to you, a special Christmas tree wish for this year. A tree that is tall and straight with boughs outstretched to shelter you from life's woes this coming year. Trimmed with love and surrounded with faith, the Christmas tree I wish for you has a bright, shining star at the top. This star will shine through the darkness around you and bring hope to the world as it did many years ago in Bethlehem. May its radiance in the days ahead flood your heart.

Under this tree, there are presents for each of you. A package filled with extraordinary memories of special people, of special times, and of other Christmas seasons from the past. While some memories may call for you to weep for times and people no longer with you, take joy in the memories of happy times and happy people. Give thanks for these happy memories and for faith in the building of new memories for the future.

Another package is filled with the peace of understanding and hope. Share that with everyone you meet and especially those dear to you. To settle for less is to make mockery of the words **Peace on earth, to men of good will.** Indeed, peace is the foundation upon which the tree I wish for you stands.

Included in my wish for you is that this tree will be part of all the good times that will be yours this season, helping to make this Christmas the merriest and most rewarding ever.

—*Howard Johnson, December 1980*

Letter to My Grandson on Graduation from High School, June 1996

Dear Grandson,

You are passing a memorable milestone in your life. It is one of many already passed and others yet to be reached. Your mother asked if I would write some *words of wisdom* for you on this occasion.

When I asked Barbara to proofread what I had written, she replied, "He's only seventeen! You should only write a short note!"

I replied, "What I have to say is too important to limit. I am certain that he will have no difficulty with it."

At seventeen, you are much wiser than most adults give you credit and much more foolish than you think you are. Time and experience usually adjust these opinions. I have a great deal to say, and on many other subjects, but will only write for you a small part of what's in my mind and heart at this time. I have two large books and many short articles in my head which are partially on paper. What I am giving you is a small part of several of these, not intended as quick reading. There is a lot which needs to be chewed thoroughly and digested to be fully understood.

When I say what I've written is important, I mean that it is important to me to say it. Whether you read it, to understand it, to believe it, to use it or not is entirely up to you. My purpose has been accomplished in the writing. It may be unimportant to you—that doesn't matter. It matters only that the effort has been made to say these things and share them with you. My father, your great-grandfather, shared many *words of wisdom* with me throughout the forty-five years we were together. He shared both the spoken and the written word. Sometimes I listened, sometimes I didn't. Though we often differed in opinion, sometimes strongly, we never lost respect for the other's opinion. I was lucky to have had such a father. Few do.

I often wish he could have known you, for he would have been so proud of you, as am I. I wish we could share more time, but life is busy for us both. Maybe in the future we can snatch a day together. I shared some precious time with my own grandfather, my mother's father, when I was twelve and then fifteen. We got to know each other during long fishing trips and while working together at the lake. The tree that now goes through the roof at the old cottage was planted by my grandfather and me when I was fifteen. He had a different view of life from my father and shared stories of his youth. He told me of traveling with a medicine show and then of running his own medicine show with an ex-slave as a sidekick. He told me many stories, some of which I'm sure were not completely true, but they were delightful tales.

Congratulations on your graduation! Well wishes for your future health, happiness, and prosperity! Prayers for the path you walk that the joys are much more than the sorrows!

With a great deal of love,

Granddad

—Howard Johnson, June 5, 1996

Too much planning is the commonest cause of defeat. The mediocre strategist conceives a plan and, like a pregnant woman, thinks the offspring of his belly, and his mood shall set a heel on destiny. A true commander's plans are changeable, adaptable, reversible, sudden, frequently surprising even to himself. They are the means that his genius seizes, to employ his full strength, at a well-considered moment, to a foreseen, unflinched from, and undeviating purpose.

—Lord Tros of Samothrace in **The Purple Pirate** by Talbot Mundy

The really dangerous people are not those who believe in violence as a means to every end or they who believe in treachery as a means to most ends. Those can be overcome by resistance and by alertness. The truly deadly menace is the intelligent man or woman whose central vision, has been indoctrinated in the accuracy and supremacy of their belief system, their view of reality. They then impose their views as controls on others. This is particularly true of many elitist intellectuals, particularly when they gain political power and control. So often they become misdirected and confused until suspicion becomes their guiding principle and pure power their only end. This is why all despots are dangerous people.

—Howard Johnson, 1992

❖   ❖   ❖

In theory, there is no difference between theory and practice. But in practice, there is.

—Yogi Berra

The difference between fiction and reality? Fiction has to make sense.

—Tom Clancy

It's not the size of the dog in the fight, it's the size of the fight in the dog.
—*Mark Twain (1835-1910)*

Victory goes to the player who makes the next-to-last mistake.
—*Chessmaster Savielly Grigorievitch Tartakower (1887-1956)*

The liberal Democrat party in the US has a record of hatred, failure, deception, corruption, and greed so blatant that only an intellectual could ignore or evade it.
—*Howard Johnson, 2009*

Bloom where you are planted.
—*Unknown*

The only power any government has is the power to crack down on criminals. Well, when there aren't enough criminals, one makes them. One declares so many things to be a crime that it becomes impossible for men to live without breaking laws.
—*Ayn Rand*

The Most Beautiful Will ever Written

I first heard *The Most Beautiful Will ever Written* in November of 1962 in Chicago at the American Dental Trade Association annual meeting in the Palmer House Hotel. Don't hold me to the date as it was a long time ago. The way it was presented was, a homeless man died on Maxwell Street, the *Bum's Row* of Chicago at the time. When he was taken to the morgue, they discovered this will in a paper in one of his pockets. The speaker had obviously taken poetic license as I learned later when I discovered the true origin of the will.

Williston Fish wrote *A Last Will* in 1897, It was published first in Harpers Weekly in 1898. Shortly afterwards it began to appear in a sporadic way in the newspapers.

From author Williston Fish:

Whenever a newspaper did not have at hand what it really wanted, which was a piece entitled 'Reunion of Brothers Separated for Fifty Years' or 'Marriage Customs Among the Natives of the Fricassee Islands' it would run in this piece of mine. In return for the free use of the piece, the paper, not to be outdone in liberality, would generally correct and change it, and fix it up, often in the most beautiful manner; so that I am forced to believe that nearly every paper has on its staff a professor of literature and belles-lettres, always ready to red-ink the essays of the beginner and give them the seeming of masterpieces and gradually to unfold to the novice all the marvels of the full college curriculum. This simple work of mine has been constantly undergoing change and improvement. Sometimes the head has been cut off; sometimes a beautiful wooden foot has been spliced on. When a certain press at Cambridge reprinted it [Cambridge is undoubtedly the home of acute belles-lettres] it used a copy in which the common word dandelions was skillfully changed to flowers, daisies was changed to blossoms, and creeks, which is only a farmer boy word, was changed to brooks. When I said that I gave "to boys all streams and ponds where one may skate," this Cambridge printer added, 'when grim winter comes.' Some writers can boast that their works have been translated into all foreign languages, but when I look pathetically about for some little boast, I can only say that this one of my pieces has been translated into all the idiot tongues of English.

The name, Charles Lounsbury, of the devisor in the will, is a name in my family of three generations ago back in York State where the real owner of it was a big, strong, all-around good kind of a man. I had an uncle, a lawyer, in Cleveland named after him, Charles Lounsbury Fish, who was a most burly and affectionate giant himself and who took delight in keeping the original Charles Lounsbury's memory green. He used to tell us of his feats of strength: that he would lift a barrel by the chimes and. drink from the bung-hole, and that in the old York State summer days he used to swing his mighty cradle, undoubtedly a *turkey-wing,* and cut a swath like a boulevard through incredible acres of yellow grain. His brain, my uncle always added, was equal to his brawn, and he had a way of winning friends and admirers as easy and comprehensive as taking a census. So I took the name of Charles Lounsbury to add strength and good will to my story.

WILLISTON FISH

Charles Lounsbury was stronger and cleverer, no doubt, than other men, and in many broad lines of business he had grown rich, until his wealth exceeded exaggeration. One morning, in his office, he directed a request to his confidential lawyer to come to him in the afternoon as he intended to have his will drawn. A will is a solemn matter, even with men whose life is given up to business, and who are by habit mindful of the future. After giving this direction he took up no other matter, but sat at his desk alone and in silence.

It was a day when summer was first new. The pale leaves upon the trees were starting forth upon the yet unbending branches. The grass in the parks had a freshness in its green like the freshness of the blue in the sky and of the yellow of the sun, a freshness to make one wish that life might renew its youth. The clear breezes from the south wantoned about, and then were still, as if loath to go finally away. Half idly, half thoughtfully, the rich man wrote upon the white paper before him, beginning what he wrote with capital letters, such as he had not made since, as a boy in school, he had taken pride in his skill with the pen:

A LAST WILL

I, CHARLES LOUNSBURY, being of sound and disposing mind and memory [he lingered on the word memory], do now make and publish this my last will and testament, in order, as justly as I may, to distribute my interests in the world among succeeding men.

And first, that part of my interests which is known among men and recognized in the sheep-bound volumes of the law as my property, being inconsiderable and of none account, I make no account of in this my will.

My right to live, it being but a life estate, is not at my disposal, but, these things excepted, all else in the world I now proceed to devise and bequeath.

Item: And first, I give to good fathers and mothers, but in trust for their children, nevertheless, all good little words of praise and all quaint pet names, and I charge said parents to use them justly, but generously, as the needs of their children shall require.

Item: I leave to children exclusively, but only for the life of their childhood, all and every the dandelions of the fields and the daisies thereof, with the right to play among them freely, according to the custom of children, warning them at the same time against the thistles. And I devise to children the yellow shores of creeks and the golden sands beneath the waters thereof, with the dragon-flies that skim the surface of said waters, and the odors of the willows that dip into said waters, and the white clouds that float high over the giant trees.

And I leave to children the long, long days to be merry in, in a thousand ways, and the night and the Moon and the train of the Milky Way to wonder at, but subject, nevertheless, to the rights hereinafter given to lovers; and I give to each child the right to choose a star that shall be his, and I direct that the child's father shall tell him the name of it, in order that the child shall always remember the name of that star after he has learned and forgotten astronomy.

Item: I devise to boys jointly all the useful idle fields and commons where ball may be played, and all snow-clad hills where one may coast, and all streams and ponds where one may skate, to have and to hold the same for the period of their boyhood. And all meadows, with the clover blooms and butterflies thereof; and all woods, with their appurtenances of squirrels and whirring birds and echoes and strange noises; and all distant places which may be visited, together with the adventures there found, I do give to said boys to be theirs. And I give to said boys each his own place at the fireside at night, with all pictures that may be seen in the burning wood or coal, to enjoy without let or hindrance and without any incumbrance of cares.

Item: To lovers I devise their imaginary world, with whatever they may need, as the stars of the sky, the red, red roses by the wall, the snow of the hawthorn, the sweet strains of music, or aught else they may desire to figure to each other the lasting-ness and beauty of their love.

Item: To young men jointly, being joined in a brave, mad crowd, I devise and bequeath all boisterous, inspiring sports of rivalry. I give to them the disdain of weakness and undaunted confidence in their own strength. Though they are rude and rough, I leave to them alone the power of making lasting friendships and of possessing companions, and to them exclusively I give all merry songs and brave choruses to sing, with smooth voices to troll them forth.

Item: And to those who are no longer children, or youths, or lovers, I leave memory, and I leave to them the volumes of the poems of Burns and Shakespeare, and of other poets, if there are others, to the end that they may live the old days over again freely and fully, without tithe or diminution; and to those who are no longer children, or youths, or lovers, I leave, too, the knowledge of what a rare, rare world it is.

*　　*　　*

I have my warts. I sometimes say things that get me in trouble. In other words, I lead with my mouth and not my head. I hate Republicans. I hate Conservatives. I hate Rush Limbaugh.

—*Howard Dean, chairman, Democrat National Committee*
from 2005 to 2009

The forever closed mind of the fundamentalist sees, hears, and understands only that which fits within the boundaries of the belief system imposed ruthlessly by outside forces and inner slavery. Such minds are usually joyless, cynical, and filled with hate for those able to think outside the box. They are mental and spiritual lemmings following other followers, even to their deaths.

—*Howard Johnson*

Rational thoughts are the precursors to good. Irrational thoughts lead invariably to evil.
—*Epictetus (55-135 A.D.)*

Patriotism has been called the last refuge of scoundrels, but anti-patriotism truly is much more so. Those who accuse opponents of any kind as using patriotism to hide their false intent are often the true scoundrels. False patriots are quite obvious to open minds.
—*Howard Johnson July 4, 2011*

A wise and frugal Government, which shall restrain men from injuring one another, which shall leave them otherwise free to regulate their own pursuits of industry and improvement, and shall not take from the mouth of labor the bread it has earned. This is the sum of good government, and this is necessary to close the circle of our felicities.
—*Thomas Jefferson*

Suppose you were an idiot, and suppose you were a member of Congress; but I repeat myself.
—*Mark Twain*

He has all the virtues I dislike and none of the vices I admire.
—*Sir Winston Churchill (1874-1965)*

Write drunk; edit sober. —*Ernest Hemingway (1899-1961)*

I criticize by creation - not by finding fault. —*Cicero (106-43 B.C.)*

The optimist proclaims that we live in the best of all possible worlds, and the pessimist fears this is true.
—*James Branch Cabell*

Sleep is an excellent way of listening to an opera.
—*James Stephens (1882-1950)*

Significant Quotes of Talbot Mundy
from: *Tros of Samothrace* and *The Purple Pirate*
Most are from the log of Lord Captain Tros of Samothrace.

It never was my view that women are the worse for audacity. To be mothers of sons worth weaning, they should have the manly virtues in addition to the qualities that charm and tempt.

Manners? They are like a cloak that either illustrates its wearer's self-respect or masks his vileness, popinjays his vices, or reveals his taste. I have observed that decent manners are invariable befitting the occasion, blunt and direct when causes are at issue, civil to the verge of gentleness where nothing but another's momentary comfort is at stake. Too-smooth manners in the face of issues is a sign of fear or treachery or weakness or of all three.

I know of no justification for the wars that men wage on one another. On the other hand, I know no reason and perceive no wisdom in the floods and famines, pestilence and earthquakes, fire and hurricane, which priests say the gods devise.

If a friend in friendship errs, it is vile to retaliate. Regret is stupid. Recrimination is a waste of time and breath. There is nothing to be done but to redeem the error. Friendship is not measurable by an error—no—no matter how great or how disastrous.

A man may be a murderer and faithful. Many are. A man may be a courtier and faithful. Some are. But the courtier-murderer, disarmed and faced with the alternative of cold steel in his throat, will babble all he knows to avoid the kind of death he has meted out to others. But first, disarm him. Armed, he believes himself an honorable man. Disarmed, he knows he has no honor.

They who laugh at a commander's failure usually lack ability or will to understand the nature of his problem. Detail, detail, detail—each dependent on another's or a hundred others' loyalty, devotion, skill, intelligence, obedience, and health. One sick man, fretting faithfully to do his stint, unknowingly unknown, may wreck a well-imagined strategy before its details unfold. I have heard self-styled critics speak . . . aye, and I have read the books of some historians who write, as if a warship can put to sea without a thousand cares first well attended. And if a ship, what of a fleet? What of an army? It is a pity, for their foes' sake, that some critics are not taken at their own evaluation and entrusted with command.

When I ask myself, as I think all thoughtful men inevitably do, have I done my duty? Have I acted manly? I perceive it is impossible for oneself to answer. That is something that only other men can do until the gods' day comes to issue judgment—aye, and beware of flattery! Man's speech is seldom sheeted close to truth's wind. But their deeds are eloquent. So that when ignorant dogs of bawdy seamen, who I have shepherded and thrashed and loved and led, behave like loyal comrades behind my back, then I take comfort. My men shall judge me. Gods, if gods there be, may judge me by the good foul-weather friends who have stood by.

It was the sea, with its roaring rage and smiling treachery, that taught me sometimes to appear to yield. Many a time I have luffed and let an enemy believe me to be beaten. I have avoided battle. I have run. But I have never struck my flag. Storm lover though I have ever been, and conqueror of storms though I have had to be . . . aye, though I pray for a storm if I must meet an enemy at sea . . . I see no wisdom in opposing storm and enemy. Rather, I use the one to help me defeat the other. And if it seems advisable, I run from both to await my moment.

Certain philosophers, some priests, and many women have accused me of loving war. I hate it. I despise it as an arbiter of quarrels. Would that my intelligence and vigor might be put to a more creative use. But I have seen that they, whose speech is most contemptuous of warriors, are also they whose blunders, acrimony, ignorance, and malice aggravate the quarrels that produce war. To avoid war, for the sake of friendship—aye, to prevent a quarrel—I am willing to risk all that I have and to forego my own ambition. But I will yield to no tyrant. And when I find myself at war, I choose to win.

Two heads are better than one, and three than two, but when a plan is reached, let there be one commander. One only. Let the others obey. I would rather obey a man, whose talent for command I thought inferior to mine, than make the unwise effort to attempt to share authority.

The one test of a commander's competence is battle, no other. There is no denying a defeat. No argument annuls a victory.

The incomparable depth of stupidity is that of the commander who does that which his enemy expects because tradition justifies it. The only time when traditional strategy and tactics are fit to employ is when the enemy expects something else and therefore mistakes old methods for a ruse.

It is unwise to expect a clever opportunist to obey, if given opportunity to disobedience to serve himself. Your aims, your plans—aye, and your dangers also, should he know them—would be the natural means by which he would secretly seek to advance himself, inevitably to your cost and perhaps your ruin. There is one wise way, and only one, to make use of such men. Study their natural cunning, as the hunter studies animals, in order to be able to predict their probable behavior when free to follow their inclination.

Money to pay for provisions is more important to a ship's commander than the wind. He can wait for a fair wind. He can hunt a lee in stormy weather. But unless he can pay for supplies, there is no alternative but piracy, disguised or open. And whoever thinks that pirates avoid paying for their depredations is either very ignorant or void of common sense.

It is not the unpredictables that govern issues. It is the steady, unwavering day-by-day persistent exercise of judgment, always hewing nearer to the line of wisdom. Far though it may be from wisdom, yet that effort rarefies its maker's thought until he fits himself for swift and right decision in emergencies that baffle them who envision only purpose and let wisdom wait, as if it were not, or as if it were a poet's word for something unattainable or unknown.

Half of human history was made by drunkards in their cups and written down by slaves of one imposter or another in the hope of table leavings.

I was born and taught upon the threshold of the holy mystery, and all my days I have been faithful to the duty laid upon me to pursue peace . . . aye, and to forego my own advantage if thereby peace might come. But I have found no peace on earth or any honorable way of avoiding war.

It is better to be feared than loved, if you cannot be both.
>—*Niccolo Machiavelli (1469-1527), The Prince*

Whatever is begun in anger ends in shame.
>—*Benjamin Franklin (1706-1790)*

The President has kept all of the promises he intended to keep.
>—*Clinton aide George Stephanopolous speaking on Larry King Live*

We're going to turn this team around 360 degrees.
>—*Jason Kidd, upon his drafting to the Dallas Mavericks*

Half this game is ninety percent mental. —*Yogi Berra*

There is only one nature - the division into science and engineering is a human imposition, not a natural one. Indeed, the division is a human failure; it reflects our limited capacity to comprehend the whole. —*Bill Wulf*

There's many a bestseller that could have been prevented by a good teacher.
>—*Flannery O'Connor (1925-1964)*

Notable Quotes from the NIV Bible

Those who discount the Bible because of religion, or because it is a religious work, deny themselves learning a great deal of ageless knowledge collected and preserved for thousands of years. This knowledge, mostly about human behavior and about interacting profitably and successfully with others, is real, practical, and valuable. A great many life rules and lessons explained and demonstrated, apply to almost any human situation. Here are a few excerpts from the Bible that apply across the scope of human actions.

—Howard Johnson

The proverbs of Solomon, son of David, king of Israel: For attaining wisdom and discipline; for understanding words of insight; for acquiring a disciplined and prudent life, doing what is right and just and fair; for giving prudence to the simple, knowledge and discretion to the young—let the wise listen and add to their learning, and let the discerning get guidance—for understanding proverbs and parables, the sayings and riddles of the wise. The fear of the LORD is the beginning of knowledge, but fools despise wisdom and discipline. Listen, my son, to your father's instruction and do not forsake your mother's teaching. They will be a garland to grace your head and a chain to adorn your neck.

—Proverbs 1:1–9

Moreover, no man knows when his hour will come: as fish are caught in a cruel net, or birds are taken in a snare, so men are trapped by evil times that fall unexpectedly upon them.

—Ecclesiastes 9:12

Blessed is the man who finds wisdom, the man who gains understanding, for she is more profitable than silver and yields better returns than gold. She is more precious than rubies; nothing you desire can compare with her. Long life is in her right hand; in her left hand are riches and honor. Her ways are pleasant ways, and all her paths are peace. She is a tree of life to those who embrace her; those who lay hold of her will be blessed. By wisdom the LORD laid the earth's foundations, by understanding He set the heavens in place; by His knowledge the deeps were divided, and the clouds let drop the dew. My son, preserve sound judgment and discernment, do not let them out of your sight; they will be life for you, an ornament to grace your neck.

—Proverbs 3:13–22

Wisdom calls aloud in the street, she raises her voice in the public squares; at the head of the noisy streets she cries out, in the gateways of the city she makes her speech: "How long will you simple ones love your simple ways? How long will mockers delight in mockery and fools hate knowledge? If you had responded to my rebuke, I would have poured out my heart to you and made my thoughts known to you. But since you rejected me when I called and no one gave heed when I stretched out my hand, since you ignored all my advice and would not accept my rebuke, I in turn will laugh at your disaster; I will mock when calamity overtakes you—when calamity overtakes you like a storm, when disaster sweeps over you like a whirlwind, when distress and trouble overwhelm you.

"Then they will call to me but I will not answer; they will look for me but will not find me. Since they hated knowledge and did not choose to fear the LORD, since they would not accept my advice and spurned my rebuke, they will eat the fruit of their ways and be filled with the fruit of their schemes. For the waywardness of the simple will kill them, and the complacency of fools will destroy them, but whoever listens to me will live in safety and be at ease, without fear of harm."

My son, if you accept my words and store up my commands within you, turning your ear to wisdom and applying your heart to understanding, and if you call out for insight and cry aloud for understanding, and if you look for it as for silver and search for it as for hidden treasure, then you will understand the fear of the LORD and find the knowledge of God. *—Proverbs 1:20-33 & 2:1-5*

I also saw under the sun this example of wisdom that greatly impressed me: There was once a small city with only a few people in it. And a powerful king came against it, surrounded it and built huge siege works against it. Now there lived in that city a man poor but wise, and he saved the city by his wisdom. But nobody remembered that poor man. So I said, "Wisdom is better than strength." But the poor man's wisdom is despised, and his words are no longer heeded. *—Ecclesiastes 9:13-16*

The quiet words of the wise are more to be heeded than the shouts of a ruler of fools. Wisdom is better than weapons of war, but one sinner destroys much good.
—Ecclesiastes 9:17-18

Enjoy life with your wife, whom you love, all the days of this meaningless life that God has given you under the sun—all your meaningless days. For this is your lot in life and in your toilsome labor under the sun. Whatever your hand finds to do, do it with all your might, for in the grave, where you are going, there is neither working nor planning nor knowledge nor wisdom. *—Ecclesiastes 9:9-10*

(Read also the King James, following)

Notable Quotes from the KJV Bible

Live joyfully with the wife whom thou lovest all the days of the life of thy vanity, which he hath given thee under the sun, all the days of thy vanity: for that is thy portion in this life, and in thy labour which thou takest under the sun. Whatsoever thy hand findeth to do, do it with thy might; for there is no work, nor device, nor knowledge, nor wisdom, in the grave, whither thou goest.
(Read also the NIV, Page 21) —*Ecclesiastes 9:9-10, KJV*

A continual dropping in a very rainy day and a contentious woman are alike. Whosoever hideth her hideth the wind, and the ointment of his right hand, which betrayeth itself.

—Proverbs 27:15-16, KJV

A foolish son is the calamity of his father: and the contentions of a wife are a continual dropping. House and riches are the inheritance of fathers: and a prudent wife is from the LORD.

—Proverbs 19:13-14, KJV

It is better to dwell in a corner of the housetop, than with a brawling woman in a wide house.

—Proverbs 21:9, KJV

Truly the light is sweet, and a pleasant thing it is for the eyes to behold the sun: But if a man live many years, and rejoice in them all; yet let him remember the days of darkness; for they shall be many. All that cometh is vanity.

—Ecclesiastes 11:7-8, KJV

Rejoice, O young man, in thy youth, and let thy heart cheer thee in the days of thy youth, and walk in the ways of thine heart, and in the sight of thine eyes: but know thou, that for all these things God will bring thee into judgment. Therefore remove sorrow from thy heart, and put away evil from thy flesh: for childhood and youth are vanity

—Ecclesiastes 11: 9-10, KJV

Who can find a virtuous woman? for her price is far above rubies. The heart of her husband doth safely trust in her, so that he shall have no need of spoil. She will do him good and not evil all the days of her life. She seeketh wool, and flax, and worketh willingly with her hands. She is like the merchants' ships; she bringeth her food from afar. She riseth also while it is yet night, and giveth meat to her household, and a portion to her maidens. She considereth a field, and buyeth it: with the fruit of her hands she planteth a vineyard. She girdeth her loins with strength, and strengtheneth her arms. She perceiveth that her merchandise is good: her candle goeth not out by night. She layeth her hands to the spindle, and her hands hold the distaff. She stretcheth out her hand to the poor; yea, she reacheth forth her hands to the needy. She is not afraid of the snow for her household: for all her household are clothed with scarlet. She maketh herself coverings of tapestry; her clothing is silk and purple. Her husband is known in the gates, when he sitteth among the elders of the land. She maketh fine linen, and selleth it, and delivereth girdles unto the merchant. Strength and honour are her clothing, and she shall rejoice in time to come. She openeth her mouth with wisdom, and in her tongue is the law of kindness. She looketh well to the ways of her household, and eateth not the bread of idleness. Her children arise up, and call her blessed; her husband also, and he praiseth her. Many daughters have done virtuously, but thou excellest them all. Favour is deceitful, and beauty is vain: but a woman that feareth the LORD, she shall be praised. Give her of the fruit of her hands, and let her own works praise her in the gates.

—*Proverbs 31:10–31, KJV*

Make a joyful noise unto the LORD, all ye lands. Serve the LORD with gladness: come before his presence with singing. Know ye that the LORD he is God: it is he that hath made us, and not we ourselves; we are his people, and the sheep of his pasture. Enter into his gates with thanksgiving, and into his courts with praise: be thankful unto him, and bless his name. For the LORD is good; his mercy is everlasting, and his truth endureth to all generations

—*Psalm 100, KJV*

I have not failed. I've just found 10,000 ways that won't work.

—*Thomas Alva Edison (1847-1931)*

Political correctness is tyranny with manners.

—*Charlton Heston (1924-2008)*

You can avoid reality, but you cannot avoid the consequences of avoiding reality.

—*Ayn Rand (1905-1982)*

Here are a few suggestions for a more pleasant and enjoyable life.

Recognize that life is never fair. Most of it is a random process.

Never look back. They may be gaining on you.

Once you've fallen in love, never stop loving that person.

Dream all the wild dreams you can dream, but plan and decide rationally.

Always show everyone you care about, even your pet, that you love them.

Use emotions for love. Use logic for decisions.

Savor and cultivate pleasant emotions. Minimize and weed out unpleasant ones.

Laugh every day, even if you don't feel like there is anything to laugh about.

Take frequent walks—through the woods if possible.

Get rid of everything you don't need or that doesn't hold treasured memories.

Use your last cent to buy a flower for someone.

Each and every day, share a treasured memory with someone you care about.

Tell everyone just how special your special someone is, and do it at every chance you get..

Consider that every statement you make to anyone is a commitment to make it true.

Never lose that child-like wonder at the world. Keep it alive and active.

Rid yourself of everything that is not useful, beautiful, joyful, or filled with wonder.

Forgive everyone of everything and especially discard grudges.

If you have a dog, give it all the love you can and as much freedom as possible.

Say something pleasant to everyone you meet every day.

—Howard Johnson, 2011

A strong body makes the mind strong. As to the species of exercises, I advise the gun. While this gives moderate exercise to the body, it gives boldness, enterprise and independence to the mind. Games played with the ball, and others of that nature, are too violent for the body and stamp no character on the mind. Let your gun therefore be your constant companion of your walks.

—Thomas Jefferson

Sex and religion are closer to each other than either might prefer.
—*Saint Thomas More (1478-1535)*

Religion and politics are closer to each other than either might prefer.
—*Howard Johnson, 2008*

How wrong it is for a woman to expect the man to build the world she wants, rather than to create it herself.
—*Anais Nin (1903-1977)*

Don't be so humble - you are not that great.
—*Golda Meir (1898-1978) to a visiting diplomat*

What Is Love and What Is It About

Love is a word used to describe and define an almost infinite number of sets of emotions related to a sense of strong affection and attachment. The word love can refer to an endless variety of types of feelings, states of mind, feelings of the heart, and attitudes, ranging from generic pleasure —"I love that suit," to intense, personal devotion and attraction —"I love my spouse." This wide and varied range of feelings, uses, and meanings make *love* impossible to define out of context. The intense variations and complex nature of the reactions and feelings associated with *love* make it wide ranging and extremely difficult to communicate or understand. In many instances, it is such a broad and nebulous thing it defies description and even comparison to other emotional states.

In most instances, it comes from the deepest instinctual, almost primordial parts of our being. Because of this, it can bring individuals to do incredibly beautiful as well as terribly evil things. The dedication and self sacrifice of love is frequently equaled on the dark side by cruel and evil acts. This powerful force of central psychological importance is one of the most common themes in the creative arts. Our literature is filled with love themes from the earliest writings, both fictional and true. The quotes in the section to follow spans the width and depth of love, mostly romantic love between a man and a woman.
—*Howard Johnson 2009*

When only cops have guns, it's called *a police state*.
—*Robert Heinlein*

Greek words for love:

* Eros (ě???éros) is passionate love, with sensual desire and longing. The Modern Greek word *erotas* means *(romantic) love*. However, eros does not have to be sexual in nature. Eros can be interpreted as a love for someone whom you love more than the philial love of friendship. It can also apply to dating relationships as well as marriage. Plato refined his own definition. Although eros is initially felt for a person, with contemplation it becomes an appreciation of the beauty within that person, or even becomes appreciation of beauty itself. It should be noted Plato does not talk of physical attraction as a necessary part of love, hence the use of the word platonic to mean, *without physical attraction*. Plato also said eros helps the soul recall knowledge of beauty and contributes to an understanding of spiritual truth. Lovers and philosophers are all inspired to seek truth by eros. The most famous ancient work on the subject of eros is Plato's Symposium, which is a discussion among the students of Socrates on the nature of eros.

* Philia (f??a philía), which means friendship in modern Greek, a dispassionate virtuous love, was a concept developed by Aristotle. It includes loyalty to friends, family, and community and requires virtue, equality and familiarity. In ancient texts, philia denoted a general type of love, used for love between family, between friends, a desire or enjoyment of an activity, as well as between lovers. This is the only other word for *love* used in the ancient text of the New Testament besides agape, but even then it is used substantially less frequently.

* Agape (ἀ??p? agápe) means *love* in modern day Greek, such as in the term s'agapo (S'a?ap?), which means *I love you*. In Ancient Greek it often refers to a general affection rather than the attraction suggested by *eros*; agape is used in ancient texts to denote feelings for a good meal, for one's children, and for a spouse. It can be described as the feeling of being content or holding one in high regard. The verb appears in the New Testament describing, amongst other things, the relationship between Jesus and the beloved disciple. In biblical literature, its meaning and usage is illustrated by self-sacrificing, giving love to all--both friend and enemy.

It is used in Matthew 22:39, "Love your neighbour as yourself," and in John 15:12, "This is my commandment, that you love one another as I have loved you," and in 1 John 4:8, "God is love."

However, the word *agape* is not always used in the New Testament in a positive sense. II Timothy 4:10 uses the word in a negative sense. The Apostle Paul writes," For Demas hath forsaken me, having loved (agapo) this present world...." Thus the word *agape* is not always used of a divine love or the love of God. Christian commentators have expanded the original Greek definition to encompass a total commitment or self-sacrificial love for the thing loved. Because of its frequency of use in the New Testament, Christian writers have developed a significant amount of theology based solely on the interpretation of this word.

* Storge (st???? storge) means *affection* in modern Greek; it is natural affection, like that felt by parents for offspring. Rarely used in ancient work and then almost exclusively as a descriptor of relationships within the family.

Poems of and about Love

It is not, Celia, within our power to say how long our love will last;
It may be within this hour may lose those joys we now do taste.
The blessed that immortal be, from change in love are only free.
Then since we mortal lovers are, ask not how long our love will last,
But while it does, let us take care each minute be with pleasure passed:
Were it not madness to deny to live because we're sure to die?

—*George Etheridge*

Memory is the power to gather roses in winter, snowflakes in July, and to taste a loving kiss from long ago.

—*Howard Johnson, 1970*

To say that one will perish without love does not mean that everyone without adequate love dies. Many do, for without love the will to live is often impaired to such an extent that a person's resistance is critically lowered and death follows. But most of the time, lack of love makes people depressed, anxious, and without zest for life. They remain lonely and unhappy, without friends or work they care for, their life a barren treadmill, stripped of all creative action and joy.

—*Smiley Blanton*

A First Impression - Cool, devastating eyes across the room. Drawing . . . attracting. Deep, poised eyes, searching . . . reaching. Lean, taut body moving catlike, possessing space, not using it. Finely chiseled face, controlled smile—exotic, mysterious, promise of depth.

—*Howard Johnson, 1982*

The human heart has hidden treasures, in secret kept, in silence sealed; the thoughts, the hopes, the dreams, the pleasures, whose charms were broken if revealed.

– *Charlotte Bronte*

Love me not for comely grace, for my pleasing eye or face;
Nor for my outward part, no, nor for a constant heart:
For these may fail or turn to ill, so thou and I shall sever.
Keep, therefore, a true woman's eye,
And love me still, but know not why;
So hast thou the same reason still
To dote on me ever.

—George Etheridge, 1635-1691

O! let me have thee whole,—all—all—be mine!
That shape, the fairness, that sweet minor zest
Of love, your kiss,—those hands, those eyes divine,
That warm, white, lucent, million-pleasured breast,—

—John Keats

Oh, the comfort, the inexpressible comfort of feeling safe with a person; having neither to weigh thoughts nor measure words, but to pour them all out, just as they are, chaff and grain together, knowing that a faithful hand will take and sift them, keep what is worth keeping, and then, with the breath of kindness, blow the rest away.

—George Elliott

The artist is nothing without the gift, but the gift is nothing without work.

—Emile Zola (1840-1902)

It's wonderful to have someone who really understands . . .
Someone who gives the tenderness your heart sorely demands . . .
Someone to tell your troubles to when evening lights are low . . .
Who with a smile can drive away the dreary clouds of woe . . .
Understanding is a treasure gold can never buy . . .
For it has a magic power to lift the spirit high . . .
Those who proceed without it lose out at every turn . . .
Like souls adrift upon life's sea they will ever yearn . . .
So if you have someone, love them with all your heart . . .
For understanding people are few and far apart!

—Smiley Blanton

LOVE - IMPRESSIONS

Love is a passion of the heart, the soul, and the body. When new, it quickens the heartbeat, excites the soul, and stimulates one physically and mentally. It brings about intense desire to be with the one loved, great joy when together, and intense longing when apart. There is no antidote without mental anguish, no relief without deep sense of loss, no cessation without intense pain. Even when not returned in kind, it causes one to smile constantly and weep tears of pure joy until it fades away. It is a powerful and motivating force for good when well directed.

As the years pass, its burning intensity is gradually replaced by deep feelings of comfort and warmth of the soul and heart. It gets better and better, only ending in the final, tragic parting that brings such terrible pain. For these reasons, love is not the domain of cowards. It takes genuine bravery to risk it. Such is love and the price we must someday pay for loving even until that final moment—pain. Fear of that pain cannot stop me from loving deeply and sincerely—even at an advanced age.

—*Howard Johnson, 2006 at age 78*

This book fills a much-needed gap.

—*Moses Hadas (1900-1966) in a review*

The full use of your powers along lines of excellence.

—*definition of happiness by John F. Kennedy (1917-1963)*

Only two things are infinite, the universe and human stupidity, and I'm not sure about the former.

—*Albert Einstein (1879-1955)*

It is not in the stars to hold our destiny but in ourselves.

—*William Shakespeare*

An untruth that conveys a true meaning from one person to another is, in fact, a truth—a truth that conveys a false meaning is in fact an untruth. Truth or untruth is not in the medium, only in the message!

—*Howard Johnson, 1968*

There is only one danger I find in life. One may take too many precautions.

—*Alfred Adler*

If a man does his best, what else is there?
—*General George S. Patton (1885-1945*

I do not feel obliged to believe that the same God who has endowed us with sense, reason, and intellect has intended us to forgo their use.
—*Galileo Galilei (1564-1642)*

I found solace in nursing a pervasive sense of grievance and animosity against my mother's race. There was something about her that made me wary, a little too sure of herself, maybe and white.
—*From Dreams of my Father - Barack Hussein Obama*

The real, the sweetest taste of victory comes when you win in your adversary's battlefield, fought with his weapons and his set of rules at a time of his choosing, when losing would cost you no loss of stature. Even more so when you are your own adversary!
—*Howard Johnson, 1972*

I am familiar with the arguments of priests whose truth I vigorously doubt because they take for granted claims impossible to prove. I am equally familiar with the logic that denies all speculative thought, as if a midnight to a midnight were the limit of existence, and a man no more important than a louse. I find the one as superstitious as the other, and, of the two, perhaps the priests less stupid.
—*Lord Tros of Samothrace - Talbot Mundy*

You may not be interested in war, but war is interested in you.
—*Leon Trotsky (1879-1940)*

Every day we should hear at least one little song, read one good poem, see one exquisite picture, and, if possible, speak a few sensible words.
— *Johann Wolfgang von Goethe*

To know a person's religion we need not listen to his profession of faith but must find his brand of intolerance.
—*Eric Hoffer*

A decision is necessary only when the facts at hand do not reveal the only course to take.
—*Howard Johnson, 1960*

Remembering Easter Sunday, 1945 - 67 years ago today.

I awakened early to what was to be a busy day. It was still dark, but the birds were announcing the day was about to begin. The first thing on my schedule was the big, downtown sunrise service at the Cleveland Public Auditorium. The Cleveland Heights High a capella choir was to sing, and I was in the second tenor section. The service was to begin at 6:30 and we were to be there no later than 6:00. I was granted the use of the family car as my parents were to be taken to our church services by some church members who were also neighbors. That meant I would have to leave home by about five in order to have time to pick up a couple of other choir members, get downtown, park, and walk to the auditorium by 6:00.

I would have picked up my steady girl, Dolores, who also sang in the choir, but her parents were attending the service and she was to go with them. The drive downtown was brightened by the clear, blue sky of a warm and gorgeous spring day. Daffodils and narcissi were blooming everywhere. Even a few early tulips were showing off their colors. One spectacular passage, Cedar Hill, was down a small gorge through the Euclid Escarpment. It was ablaze with bright yellow forsythia clinging to the sides of the gorge. The air was filled with the fresh fragrance of spring. I don't remember, but I know the birds were singing their hearts out as we drove down town.

We parked the car, walked to the auditorium, and to our dressing room in good time. After we donned our choir robes, I had the chance to talk to my sweetie. We made arrangements to meet with her and her parents when the performance was over. Soon Strick, our choir director, George F. Strickling, lined us up for a warm up before our stage entrance. I don't remember much about the concert, or even any of the songs we sang. As a teen, deeply in love, I was probably too busy trying to catch Dee's eye while we were singing. From my position in the back row on the extreme left of the semicircular arrangement of the choir, I was in her line-of-sight from where she stood in the first row on the extreme right.

I was to meet Dee and her folks after we finished and changed back into our Easter finery. We were to meet outside the side entrance. We actually ended up meeting in the hallway on our way out. One look at her in her Easter outfit and I was overwhelmed. Her bright yellow dress was set off by a spectacular, dark blue, wide-brimmed, straw hat. She was positively the most beautiful girl I had ever seen, and she was my girl. I couldn't get over looking at her. To use some of today's vernacular, she was drop-dead gorgeous. To make it even better, we were about to walk up Euclid Avenue in Cleveland's Easter Parade, me, walking with the most beautiful girl in the world. I was walking on air, proud as a young man could possibly be.

The aura of her in that gorgeous yellow dress and that spectacular hat, spun a magic spell that held me all day long. I cannot remember another thing about the middle of that day other than watching her. After her folks headed for home, Dee joined me while I took my two passengers home. Soon after we dropped the second one off, Dee carefully removed her hat as I pulled to the curb. Soon we were wrapped in an embrace and a lingering kiss. We just couldn't wait until we could park in front of her house. I remember later events clearly, sitting with her in front of 2471 Saybrook Road, sharing tender love words, and kiss after kiss until she had to go inside. Tomorrow was a school day and her curfew was 10:00.

As I drove home down Meadowbrook Boulevard, visions of the days events flashed through my mind. I was totally and deliriously in the grasp of young love, and loving every minute of it. All I could think was, how could I possibly be so lucky?

—*Howard Johnson - Easter Sunday, 2012*

God is a comedian playing to an audience too afraid to laugh.
—*Voltaire (1694-1778)*

There's no such thing as life without bloodshed. I think the notion that the species can be improved in some way, that everyone could live in harmony, is a really dangerous idea. Those who are afflicted with this notion are the first ones to give up their souls, their freedom.

—*Cormac McCarthy*

A man of knowledge is free . . .He has no honor, no dignity, no family, no country, but only life to be lived.

—*Juan Matus*

A man of heart is not free . . .He has honor, dignity, family, home, country, and love of life to be enjoyed.

—*Howard Johnson, 1971*

Natural science does not consist in ratifying what others have said, but in seeking the causes of phenomena.

—*Saint Albertus Magnus*

Seek for the patronage of some great man and, like a creeping vine on a tall tree, crawl upward where I cannot stand alone? No thank you!

Dedicate, as others do, poems to pawnbrokers? Be a buffoon in the vile hope of teasing out a smile on some cold face? No thank you!

Eat a toad for breakfast every morning? Make my knees callous and cultivate a supple spine; wear out my belly groveling in the dust? No thank you!

Scratch the back of any swine that roots up gold for me? Tickle the horns of Mammon with my left hand, while my right, too proud to know his partner's business, takes in the fee? No thank you!

Use the fire God gave me to burn incense all day long under the nose of wood or stone? No thank you!

Shall I . . . struggle to insinuate my name into the columns of the Mercury? No thank you!

Calculate, scheme, be afraid, love more to make a visit than a poem; seek introductions, favors, influences? No thank you. No thank you! And again, no thank you!

But . . . to sing, to laugh, to dream, to walk in my own way and be alone, free, with an eye to see things as they are, a voice that means manhood . . . to cock my hat where I choose, at a word, a yes, a no, to fight, or to write. To travel any road under the sun, under stars, nor doubt if fame or fortune lie beyond the bourne. Never to make a line I have not heard in my own heart; yet with all modesty to say: my soul, be satisfied with flowers, with fruit, with weeds even, but gather them in one garden you may call your own.

So when I win some triumph, by some chance, render no share to Caesar . . . in a word, I am too proud to be a parasite, and if my nature lacks the germ that grows towering to heaven like the mountain pine, or like the oak, sheltering multitudes. I stand not high it may be . . . but alone.

—*Cyrano de Bergerac*

Look to this day, for it is the life; the very life of life. In its brief course lie all the verities and realities of your existence; the bliss of growth, the glory of action, the splendor of beauty. For yesterday is but a dream and tomorrow is only a vision, but today, well lived, makes every yesterday a dream of happiness and every tomorrow a vision of hope.

Look well, therefore, to this day, such as is the salutation of the dawn.

—*from the Sanscrit*

One of My Father's Many Poems

The melancholy days are here, the saddest of the year,
When we must close the cottage and take in the pier.
The fishing tackle and the boats must be stored away
To wait the coming of spring or early summer day.
The sun is not so warm now; the breeze is very cool.
The water's getting colder in our outdoor swimming pool.
The trees have changed their colors; the leaves are coming down.
The grass is still a little green, but spots are turning brown.
But there is a certain beauty we find here in the fall.
Too bad more cannot enjoy it, even our children all.
The sky has a peculiar shade and threatens rain today,
But the sun sneaks through so often, it's really hard to say.
This summer has been wonderful, and this fall as well.
We really have enjoyed it more than we can tell.
So we are really sad when closing this lake home.
We'll come again next summer when we begin to roam.
Thank God we both enjoy good health and this kind of life,
Living close to nature and away from city strife.
For all those blessings we enjoy and for our family's love,
We will be forever thankful to our great God above.
—*Howard R. Johnson, September 8, 1954*

Too many pieces of music finish too long after the end.
—*Igor Stravinsky (1882-1971)*

Anything that is too stupid to be spoken is sung.
—*Voltaire (1694-1778)*

When choosing between two evils, I always like to try the one I've never tried before.
—*Mae West (1892-1980)*

Writers and Women
A warning for women about writers, male writers.

Beware of starting a relationship with a writer. They are human and have all the foibles, the charms, the weaknesses, the strengths, the nastiness, the kindnesses, and the frequent inconsistencies exhibited by the male of the species. That being said, there are things writers share with all artists, and a few peculiarities attributable to writers alone. All of them have a number of these sometimes pleasing and sometimes distressing traits. Many have all of them. I repeat, **all of them have a number of these sometimes pleasing and sometimes distressing traits. Many have all of them.**

Writers are Artists and thus unconventional people. They do not often follow the norms of polite society and this often puts them at odds with "normal" persons. If they follow rules they are often of their own making or at least manipulating, and do not necessarily follow society's rule book. The very few who gain fame and fortune are especially afflicted with these attributes.

Writers are frequently unkempt and unconcerned about their personal appearance, their place of residence or their workplace. Since they work alone, they do not have to worry about interference of any kind from other people. As a result they often lack social skills and can be opinionated, rude, and even uncivil.

They treat money and finances in the same manner and rarely have enough to live on. Those who inherited money or have a sponsor who provides for their needs, are the fortunate ones. When a windfall comes for any reason including getting successfully published, they give freely to friends and family. They are apt to give to groupies or other leeches who disappear as quickly as the money. Frequently, portions of their life are spent in poverty and they sometimes die penniless and alone.

Writers are emotional. Most are driven by emotion more than by rational thought. Most people share this trait, but it is greatly amplified in writers. They are known for volatile, often unpredictable actions that can become very damaging, even self destructive. Their emotions frequently override their logic, particularly in situations where the powerful emotions of love, hate, revenge, remorse, and self pity are aroused. They frequently get themselves into situations where there are no possible favorable solutions.

Those who do learn to leash in their emotions can do so up to a point. Once that point is passed, emotions can burst forth with tremendous force, drowning all rational responses.

Their lives are often erratic and in turmoil. Many are subject to most acts of debauchery and in some extreme cases, can be found in a drunken stupor in an alley or gutter. For this and other reasons, writers often die quite young. Quite a few die of drug overdoses, or by their own devices. A few die at the hands of the husband or lover of one of their conquests. They are not a good risk for life insurance or investment.

Though they often woo and marry women they love deeply, they are prone to cheat, given the opportunity. Writers have almost a magical charm. Why women start a romance with a known bounder and expect to change him is beyond understanding. Tragic stories of these foolish adventures abound in literature and folklore.

Writers have all of the vices of other artists plus a few peculiar to the species. They are trained and practiced in the art of using words to paint pictures and scenarios of imaginary people and things. They are completely unbounded by facts and are not even bound by natural laws. Science fiction writers may adhere to most of the rules of science, but fantasy writers in particular are limited only by their considerable imaginations. When their work turns out badly, what do they do? They either discard it or rewrite it. There is a common belief and saying among writers that is touted in books and lectures, "rewriting is the key to success."

That would pose no problem if it were not carried over into the writer's life experiences. What happens in real life is that the writer jumps in and acts in a similar manner to his writing. It's, "If it doesn't work out right, rewrite it!" But life cannot be "rewritten." Things once said cannot be "unsaid." The vase once broken cannot be returned to its original condition. Real life happenings cannot be "rewritten."

The situations in his stories can become quite factual and the characters in his creations become as real people to the writer. In his mind he can change things at will, hate characters or love them. He can also use his talent as a wordsmith to manipulate their lives, kill them if he so chooses, with no real consequences. He can even resurrect the ones he killed if he wants. Writers can come to view real live people the same way. They can become extremely disturbed when people don't follow their "script." There are many other problems associated with this imposition of creative writing into real life. There is one horrible true story about a writer who became so enamored with one of his heroines that he committed suicide after writing of her sudden death. That's quite obviously carrying "method writing" a bit too far.

Just think about writers as normal people whose emotions are much stronger and more able to create actions than most and who can shift into emotional hyperdrive in an instant. The writer's emotional fish story would not turn the small fish into a bigger one, but into a virtual monster.

On the positive side, writers can be quite wonderful friends or companions. They are quite sensitive and try not to be hurtful to those they care for. Emotions directed to positive action can be wonderful resulting in deep, abiding love, and unbelievable acts of kindness. They can become quite altruistic.

They are also quite sensitive and can be hurt deeply and quickly by unintentional acts. Those without the negative traits can make affectionate and loyal friends, lovers, and husbands. Ah, but finding those with all positive traits borders on the impossible. So if you take a writer into your life as a friend or lover, be prepared to accept a few warts . . . maybe lots of warts.

—*Howard Johnson, December, 2009*

❖   ❖   ❖

My worst mistakes were when I doubted my own judgement.

—*Unknown*

Perception, ah yes, perception, it is what drives our decisions, controls our emotions of love, anger, joy, disappointment, friendship, hatred, virtually everything we think or react to. Perception overrules facts, logic, and reality. Whether from love, avarice, or foolishness, and no matter how removed perception is from truth, it still rules us and determines our life decisions. We do not live in a real world, but live totally in a world created by and subject to our perceptions.

—*Howard Johnson, 1960*

When one person suffers from a delusion it is called insanity; when many people suffer from a delusion it is called religion.

—*Robert Pirsig (1948-)*

Happiness and moral duty are inseparably connected.

—*George Washington*

When one person suffers from a delusion it is called insanity; when many people suffer from a delusion it is called politics.
—*Howard Johnson, 1967*

I can write better than anybody who can write faster, and I can write faster than anybody who can write better.
—*A. J. Liebling (1904-1963)*

People demand freedom of speech to make up for the freedom of thought which they avoid.
—*Soren Aabye Kierkegaard (1813-1855)*

Give me chastity and continence, but not yet.
—*Saint Augustine (354-430)*

Not everything that can be counted counts, and not everything that counts can be counted.
—*Albert Einstein (1879-1955)*

Hold yourself responsible for a higher standard than anybody expects of you. Never excuse yourself. Never pity yourself. Be a hard taskmaster to yourself and be lenient with everybody else.
—*Henry Ward Beecher*

We are all atheists about most of the gods humanity has ever believed in. Some of us just go one god further.
—*Richard Dawkins (1941-)*

On Prayer (From the Sermon on the Mount)

[5] And when you pray, do not be like the hypocrites, for they love to pray standing in the synagogues and on the street corners to be seen by men. I tell you the truth; they have received their reward in full.

[6] But when you pray, go into your room, close the door and pray to your Father, who is unseen. Then your Father, who sees what is done in secret, will reward you.

[7] And when you pray, do not keep on babbling like pagans, for they think they will be heard because of their many words.

[8] Do not be like them, for your Father knows what you need before you ask him.
—*Matthew 6:5–8 NIV*

Relativity and a Totally New Concept of Our Universe
A completely new and different way of envisioning our universe

Howard Johnson

In 1905, Albert Einstein published his first dissertation on his new Theory of Relativity. This theory was hardly noticed when he first published it. Among its new concepts, it proposed the path of light is bent or curved by gravity, in particular the powerful force of gravity exerted by large objects like the sun, black holes, or groups of galaxies.

On July 6, 1918, the following comment by Sir Arthur Eddington was published in *Scientific American Supplement*, "The position we have now reached is known as the principle of relativity. In so far as it is a physical theory, it seems to be amply confirmed by numerous experiments (except in regard to gravitation)."

The theory put forth in the 1916 paper lacked experimental proof. Several astronomers, including Arthur Stanley Eddington, in charge of Cambridge Observatory, used a solar eclipse of May 29, 1919, as an opportunity to test one prediction: light rays from a star would be bent as they passed close by the gravitational field of the sun. When the prediction appeared to be proven accurate, Einstein was hailed by the science community and achieved almost an apotheosis in the public mind. The following is an excerpt from the *Scientific American Supplement* of December 6, 1919:

"The results of the total solar eclipse of May 29 last were reported at a meeting of the Royal Astronomical Society, held on November 6. These results were most satisfactory. The star images are well defined, and the resulting shift at the limb is 1.98". That indicates a probable error of 0.12". This result agrees closely with Einstein's prediction of 1.75". It was acknowledged at the meeting that this agreement went far to establish his theory as an objective reality."

I am an amateur cosmologist and claim no fame or special expertise to back up my own theory, a concept developed over many years of thought on the subject. For this reason, I am presenting my theory as a thought-provoking variation on the accepted theory of how the universe operates. It is a combination and simplification of the many theories and ideas proposed over the years concerning the speed of light, the expansion of the universe (as conceived from information on red shifts of distant galaxies), the relation between gravity and the speed of light, and the perceptions we seem to take for granted as true and factual. It is important to recognize perception is reality to most people. The perception of the absolute linearity of light to the mammalian eye is the basis for our sense of space and time whether it is true or not. Humans and some primates are the only ones who can understand the spacial displacement of light passed through lenses and reflected by mirrors.

Add to this our own extremely complex movements. Consider we are flying on a jet between Chicago and Sau Paulo. (1) We are moving in an arc (roughly) near the surface of the earth. (2) We are moving in a circle around the earth's center of rotation. (3) This center of rotation is moving in an elliptical path around the sun. (4) The same center of rotation is moving in another elliptical path (roughly) determined by the rotation of the galaxy. (5) The center of rotation of the galaxy is moving in another path determined by the galaxy's gravitational attraction to the rest of the universe diminishing roughly as the inverse square of the distance between the center of mass of the galaxy and all of the other dispersed mass of the universe. We still haven't taken into account the gravitational effect of the moon, the Sun, the rest of the planets and asteroids, the Oort cloud, the rotating arms of the galaxy, or our position relative to the rest of the mass of the entire universe, but then who's counting? Here is the inverse square law of gravity: It obviously does not apply to light which has no mass.

$$F = \frac{Gm_1 m_2}{r^2}$$

If m_1 or $m_2 = 0$ then $F = 0$ (for light)

0 is the G force for light, no mass.

I base the reasoning for my theory on the following:

The trajectory of light is bent (the speed changes) when light passes near an object with mass. (the sun, a star, a black hole, or even a small object like the moon.) From an observer on Earth, the amount of the change is a function of two things, the speed of light, and the inverse of the cube of the distance between the center of mass of the object and the path of the light. Perhaps it never goes in a straight line, but is constantly wandering, bent by gravity as it passes by or through all kinds of collections of mass.

General relativity, or the general theory of relativity, is the geometric theory of gravitation published by Albert Einstein in 1916[1] and the current description of gravitation in modern physics. General relativity modifies and expands on special relativity and Newton's law of universal gravitation, providing a unified description of gravity as a geometric property of space and time, or spacetime. In particular, the curvature of spacetime is directly related to the energy and momentum of whatever matter and radiation are present. The relation is specified by the Einstein field equations, a system of partial differential equations.

Some predictions of general relativity differ significantly from those of classical physics, especially concerning the passage of time, the geometry of space, the motion of bodies in free fall, and the propagation of light. Examples of such differences include **gravitational time dilation, gravitational lensing, the gravitational redshift of light, and the gravitational time delay.** The predictions of general relativity have been confirmed in all observations and experiments to date. Although general relativity is not the only relativistic theory of gravity, it is the simplest theory that is consistent with experimental data. However, unanswered questions remain, the most fundamental being how general relativity can be reconciled with the laws of quantum physics to produce a complete and self-consistent theory of quantum gravity.

Einstein's theory has important astrophysical implications. For example, it implies the existence of black holes—regions of space in which space and time are distorted in such a way that nothing, not even light, can escape—as an end-state for massive stars. There is ample evidence that the intense radiation emitted by certain kinds of astronomical objects is due to black holes; for example, microquasars and active galactic nuclei result from the presence of stellar black holes and black holes of a much more massive type, respectively. The bending of light by gravity can lead to the phenomenon of gravitational lensing, in which multiple images of the same distant astronomical object are visible in the sky. General relativity also predicts the existence of gravitational waves, which have since been observed indirectly; a direct measurement is the aim of projects such as LIGO and NASA/ESA Laser Interferometer Space Antenna and various pulsar timing arrays. In addition, general relativity is the basis of current cosmological models of a consistently expanding universe.

Quote from, *Gravitational Effects on Light Propagation* **- by Joseph A. Rybczyk**

"An examination of the theoretical relationship between gravity and light propagation is presented that focuses on the role played by gravitational time dilation. Included is a fundamental model of the photon showing the interrelationship between its internal periodic behavior and a changing gravitational potential during propagation. Also presented is a fundamental discovery involving the direct relationship between the gravitational time dilation based variance in light speed and the variance in gravitational potential between two gravitational bodies or points in a gravitational field."

HJ NOTE: There are forty formulae in the entire abstract. In all of these formulae, Δ**t** is set as 0. When Δ**t** is greater than 0, all ratios relative to the force on light revert to the inverse cube rule since they are now dealing with four dimensional space. Light must be dealt with in four dimensions, otherwise the gravitational effect or force on light is zero. Actually, the gravitational effect on light is due to the curvature of space/time caused by all mass, the larger the mass, the greater the curvature. Thus the curvature caused by the mass of the entire universe is most likely visualized as the slowly pulsating surface of a sphere. This only happens in four dimensional space.

On Earth, we are in a specific location in the universe. This means our movement, relative to the universe, is infinitesimal, even over extremely long (to us) periods of time.

The universe in its entirety has an enormous mass and thus an extremely large gravitational effect. There is no question but that this affects the path and the speed of light within the universe. This is true even though the dispersion of known mass (mostly in galaxies) in the universe is lumpy and irregular.

We perceive light as traveling in a straight-line path no matter how circuitous is the actual path. Star photos taken during the May 29, 1919, eclipse proved this. The true position of those stars appearing close to the sun was different from the apparent, observed position during the eclipse. Gravitational lenses in space sometimes cause multiple images of the same objects to appear in several positions, all different from the true position. No matter what the true path light takes to reach a human observer is, the observer perceives the light to be coming directly to him in a straight line from its source. This would be true, even if the actual path were randomly distorted and irregular, spiral, helix, circle, or arc. The red-shifted galaxy we see so clearly could even be our own in the distant past where the light has circled back and intersected our current path.

Would it not be true that at a position at or near the outermost reaches of the universe, the pull or force of gravity of the entire mass of the universe would be entirely in one direction, toward the center of mass of the universe? Would this force of gravity *bend* light back into the universe, keeping it from escaping? This would, in effect, provide an event horizon for the universe, much like the event horizon of a black hole, where light cannot escape, but would be turned back into the universe. Were this the case, the visual effect on an observer within the universe would be the same as what we presently see. Our universe could even be considered similar to a ***black hole*** from which energy or matter can never escape.

If the above facts are true, all light or radiation we are aware of is traveling in a path not straight but curved because of the gravitational effect of mass—the *curvature* of the universe. At the precise point in space-time where we are now, the speed of light is relative to the masses of all objects in the universe. It is relative to the mass of planets, stars, galaxies, and the entire universe. The force of gravity (G) exerted by a mass on any other mass at any given location is proportional to the masses of the objects and inversely proportional to the square of the distance between the centers of mass of the objects. The net G force on us is a function of our position in the universe. More correctly, the ***vector sum*** of the G forces of all objects with mass in the universe. If there is a way of calculating the relationship of the mass of the universe, our position relative to such mass and its dispersion, and our measurement of the observed speed of light, it is beyond my knowledge.

If this theory is true, the universe is a finite object with a specific mass\energy value, a specific size, and a specific set of physical laws. It may or may not be expanding as the *red shift* of distant galaxies could be an effect of changes related to the position of ourselves as observers relative to the overall forces of gravity of the universe. Such being the case, there could be many other universes of varying sizes distributed throughout space-time in a fashion similar to galaxies within our universe. Energy/mass from those universes could never reach our universe, so we would never know of their existence.

I see confirmation of this overall concept in the cosmic microwave background radiation initially discovered in 1964 by Arno Penzias and Robert Wilson. They had this serendipitous finding when they were doing radio astronomy with a giant horn developed by Bell Labs for experiments with communication satellites.

Penzias recalled, "No matter where we looked, day or night, winter or summer, this background of radiation appeared everywhere in the sky. It was not tied to our galaxy, or any other known source of radio waves."

This information was confirmed and advanced by NASA's Cosmic Background Explorer or COBE satellite in 1992. Regardless of its source, this radiation was coming at us from every part of the sky in nearly the same strength. If it was generated inside the universe at any time, it meant the radiation had turned around from its outward path and was now heading toward us. This is precisely what it would do if my theory were correct.

Two narrative descriptions—more personal reflections—of my realization or creation of this theory are included in this book. These two, titled *Dream Thoughts* and *Flaglar 1037*, represent unbounded thinking, perhaps unscientific or even whimsical. I leave it to those theoretical physicists or cosmologists who know more about these things than I to apply known mathematical and physical tests to prove or disprove my theory. That is in the event they would even consider it. This would, however, provide a framework for the detailing of the relationship between the force of gravity and the speed of light. It might even lead to a better understanding and explanation of such things as the apparent accelerating red shift of faraway galaxies, dark matter, dark energy, and other theoretical creations aimed at answering cosmological questions. It certainly meshes with most of current knowledge on the subject.

More information and an update for 2008:

I seriously wonder if the astronomers and cosmologists don't have their understanding of the expansion rate of the universe backward. If, as they say, the farther a galaxy is from us, the faster it is moving away, then those galaxies farthest away from us are actually accelerating. They decided this based on measurements of the red shift of light coming from distant galaxies. The results indicate these galaxies are moving faster away than geometric expansion would indicate. Therefore, they are accelerating away from us because, as they say, the expansion rate of the universe is **accelerating**. If this is so, our universe will expand faster and faster until it disperses entirely. When the recession rate reaches the speed of light, no light from any star or galaxy will reach any other star or galaxy.

But wait a moment. The light we are measuring from those galaxies indicates they were moving away faster a billion or more years ago, much farther back in time than physically closer galaxies. If this is so, then the rate of expansion of the universe may actually be **slowing** or **decelerating.** This would also indicate the expansion will eventually slow to a stop, and the universe will start **contracting**. As some theorized a while back, this would eventually lead to a *big crunch*, an occurrence wherein matter would become pure energy and then *bounce* back as another big bang. The universe would be reborn and start over again in much the same manner as the *bounce* of matter collapse of a giant star which results in a supernova explosion. I personally believe that to be a rational theory. Proper application of this theory could counter the necessity to construct forces like *dark matter* and *dark energy* that are now so popular with theoretical cosmologists.

Not long after I wrote these last paragraphs I received the October 2008 issue of *Scientific American*. Lo and behold the title of the cover story was, **Forget the Big Bang: Now it's the Big Bounce.** It went on to describe such a scenario as I described in the earlier paragraphs and in my stories and essays written years ago. The quote, "Quantum gravity theory predicts the universe will never die," confirms my past reasoning. It then goes on to explain this new theory, similar to my own. My theory was written down first in 1992 and then expanded in 2001. It is gratifying to hear my theory at least partially confirmed, and my doubted ideas exonerated. Still, no scientist would even consider these theories coming from an unlettered amateur.

Who knows? It could become valid one day. Stranger things have happened. Oh well, at least it gave me a good feeling.

♣   ♣   ♣

It makes no sense, but to the easily led masses, **Getting even** seems preferable to the status quo even when those who do so know they are certain to be rewarded with severe loss, pain, or even death. They become one of Eric Hoffer's *True Believers*.

—*from, Energy, Convenient Solutions II by Howard Johnson, 2012*

Time goes, you say? ... ... Ah no! Alas, Time stays, we go.

— *Henry Austin Dobson*

The judgements of men are formed not from facts as they are, but as they wish them to be. They root through tons of good wheat to find three pieces of chaff if the chaff lends weight to their beliefs and argument. It is not that they want others to know the truth, but to have those others believe as they do. Beyond this, they do not care. The conceit of man ordinarily forms his criterion of truth.

—*Unknown*

Part of the $10 million I spent on gambling, part on booze and part on women. The rest I spent foolishly.

—*George Raft*

Whenever a man has cast a longing eye on offices, a rottenness begins in his conduct.

—*Thomas Jefferson*

Sailing With the Lake Tippecanoe Sailing Club

It's January 2003, and I am sitting in our dining room. A sun-brightened panorama of snow-covered ice on Lake Tippecanoe fills my view beyond the bird feeder at the window. I watch as juncos, nuthatches, house finches, sparrows, chickadees, titmice, cardinals, doves, and gold finches in winter garb flit between nearby trees and the feeders. The scene is a far cry from summer sailing, but memories of many sailing experiences on Tippy fly through my mind. When Jim Hayes first asked me to write about the sailing club, I started with a descriptive account of the club's history. Then I decided to take another, quite different tack. I would tell a story about sailing on Tippy and about the sailing club from a sailor's point of view.

My first sailing experience on Tippy was probably in 1935 when I had my first ride in a sailboat. It belonged to the family of my friend Paul Harruff on Walker's Park. Sailing all the way down past Silver Point and back was an exciting and amazing experience for a seven-year-old. The boat was immense to a small boy. It was moored to a buoy out away from shore in front of the Harruff's cottage. During the off-season, they hauled it out of the water on a large dolly running on steel rails. The rails led from the storage driveway, down to the beach and far out into the lake to where the water was at least five feet deep. I can't remember much about the boat which was probably sold or otherwise disappeared the year after my one ride. While the steel rails on the beach and yard disappeared many years ago, those submerged remained. I remember seeing them on the bottom many times while passing over in a boat. For all I know, they may still be there, lost and long forgotten.

My first actual sailing experience was in 1945 and 1946 in a Snipe owned by my friend Ed Emrick. We would sail up and down the lake picking up girls who wanted a sailboat ride. I learned how to sail all on my own because Ed preferred to sit on the deck and talk to the girls. Ah, but that's another story. My first sailboat was a molded plywood tub of a boat made by Dunphy. It had oarlocks and seats and converted into a rowboat by removal of the mast, sail, and tiller. The transom was even designed for an outboard. In it, I took my son and his entire Cub Scout pack sailing. This boat may have been slow and unwieldy, but it held many kids.

About this time, I learned about the sailboat races on Tippy. Since the Dunphy would not be suitable for racing, I acquired a used red-and-white cat-rigged boat. Soon I was racing with other small boats as a member of the sailing club. I also discovered my new boat was far too slow and unwieldy to compete. The next year, I traded it for a brand-new, bright yellow, faster and more maneuverable Barracuda. The Barracuda was a cat-rigged boat with a tall mast. I watched with undeniable envy as Harry Bishop, John Bundy, Herb Gawthrop, Jack Thompson, Jim Murray, George Buckingham, Howard Webb, Ken Zinzer, and others competed in their Lightnings—the boat to race on Tippy. It was thrilling to see a dozen or more Lightnings racing downwind, their colorful spinnakers ballooning in the following breeze. Alas, my new Barracuda was little more competitive than my previous sailboat. My enthusiasm was not dampened by my poor performance. I was definitely hooked on sailboat racing.

Determined to be a winner, I studied a book on racing and looked for a new boat that would be competitive. I found what I had been looking for, the Flying Fish, built by the maker of the Sunfish. With a planing hull, a single sail, and room for two in the cockpit, it looked like the winner it was to be. I raced the Flying Fish for several seasons, learning the thrill of my first trophy in 1969. During our Labor Day regatta, I took my oldest daughter, Deb, with me as my crew. I soon learned the extra weight was holding us back. I couldn't catch Mick Case in his Glastron. Finally, Deb abandoned ship to lighten it. An excellent swimmer and with her life jacket on, she would be safe until one of the pickup boats got to her. Now I was gaining on Mick. I knew I could catch him before the finish line, but catching Mick and passing him are two different things. One rule of sailing is that when attempting to pass, a following boat must maneuver around a leading boat. The leading boat has the right to turn up or downwind to block the boat trying to pass. The following boat must draw even with the leader to where both masts align. This is a point called *mast abeam*. The skipper of the passing boat hails the other, calling out, *mast abeam* at which point the boat being passed can no longer block. I learned several new rules of racing that day. Mick kept me at bay and won the race. I was disqualified for two infractions.

Under the able guidance of Jim Murray, the Lake Tippy Sailing Club grew with two general classes of boats racing together against boats in the same class. The *open* class included larger boats like Lightnings, Y-Flyers, E-scows, and others. Most of these boats carried both a *jib* (front sail) and a *main*, a configuration called a *sloop* rig. The other class was the *small boat* class of one-man boats with a single sail. Porpoises, Super Porpoises, Sunfish, and several others used a *lateen rig* with a single triangular sail spread between a boom at the bottom and a top spar attached at the front, all hoisted on a relatively short mast. My Flying Fish was a *cat rig* with a single sail hoisted to the top of a tall mast and with a boom at the bottom. For years, the Lightning was by far the most popular large boat while the Super Porpoise was the most popular small boat on the lake and in the races.

After several seasons with the Flying Fish, I noticed a new and completely different sailboat on the lake. This fast-moving Hobie 16 catamaran (two slender hulls with a trampoline to hold the crew) both fascinated and excited me. One windy day in July in 1971 Bruce Pierce took me out on the Tippecanoe Boat Company's Hobie. One thrilling ride and I was definitely hooked on the new boat. During one outing, we *pitch poled* twice, once throwing me through the air and far up the mast as it slammed into the water. Pitch poling is an unusual and exhilarating experience, unlike any other way of *flipping* or turning over a sailboat. Although it can happen to other sailboats, fast-moving catamarans are most likely to do so. It usually occurs during *heavy air* (relatively high winds, fifteen knots or more). The downwind hull gets buried under the water to the point where it catches in the water and virtually trips the boat, sending the prows deep into the water and the stern high into the air. The skipper and crew, usually as far back on the stern as possible, are literally catapulted through the air as the mast slams down into the water. It's a thrilling and thoroughly startling experience as it can happen so quickly.

Small Boat Regatta on Labor Day 1973

Lightning Regatta on Labor Day 1973

Sometime later, I was thrilled when he asked me to sail it whenever I liked. He wanted the new boat out on the lake, so people would see it in action and thus promote sales. During the same summer, Bruce sailed the boat in a few races. Then he asked me if I would race it for him as he was far too busy to with the marina to spend Sundays racing. This started my love affair with Hobie racing lasting more than forty active years and continuing to this day. The following season, I purchased the blue and white Hobie 16 number 1128 I had been racing for the Tippy Boat Company. I raced my Hobie for 24 summers until 1995 when a sudden windstorm destroyed it. After winning frequently in my Flying Fish, I began experiencing frequent last places in the Hobie. A different handling sailboat, the Hobie proved difficult to master for a single hull sailor. With no other Hobie racers on the lake, I had to learn by trial and error.

Pointing or sailing close to the wind is a technique of sailing as far into the wind as possible. The key is finding the balance of direction where the wind fills the tightly drawn in sails and the boat moves fairly quickly. *Point* too close into the wind and the sails will luff (flutter in the wind), and the boat will lose forward speed. Then it will stop moving as it faces directly into the wind. Sailors colorfully refer to this cessation of forward motion as *being in irons*, an ancient sailing term. Far too often, those first summers, I found myself in irons, frustrated, and watching other boats glide swiftly and cleanly past. I sometimes even backed up.

During my second summer of Hobie racing, I learned to release the jib while *coming about (*changing directions to *tack* or zigzag upwind) caused the boat to stop turning and face directly into the wind and to be dead in the water or *in irons*. By holding the jib in place until the wind caught it and pulled the boat to the opposite tack, I found the solution to the problem. Forward motion was not lost, and I saved a lots of time by using this maneuver. Within a few years, there were more Hobies on the lake than any other sailboat, maybe more than all other sailboats combined. Mick *Killer* Case started racing a Hobie. John Emrick appeared in his purple Hobie and immediately became the leading winner. About this time, the club began to use the international Portsmouth handicap system. In this system, the race committee adjusts the time of each type of boat according to its performance ability. This leveled the playing field somewhat allowing all types of sailboats to compete with a chance to win, even beating much-faster boats. This system favors the best sailors rather than the fastest boats. As the Hobies became more popular, there were enough to have a third and separate class for Hobie 16s alone. This was in addition to the large and small boat classes. Besides the Hobie 16 sailors already mentioned, there were many others over the years. These competitors include Ken and Carolyn Davidson, Jim and Verlyn Hearn, Jim and Susan Hayes, Bill Jared, George

Buckingham, Daren Baier, J. B. Van Meter, and many others no longer active or in the club. For several years, we had a small fleet of Hobie 14s raced by Ron Brown, Phil Jung, Bill Allen, and several others.

While competing, I learned the sailing techniques peculiar to racing on Tippy with its high shores and jutting points. In almost any wind, there are blind spots where those high shores change the wind direction or block it completely. Silver Point, a high bluff jutting out into the lake, creates wind shadows and eddies that must be dealt with, often as far from shore as the middle of the lake. Strong winds from the southwest create rotating horizontal cells that roll well out into the lake. One picture in particular demonstrates the unbelievable effects of one of these invisible cells. In it, two Lightings—one skippered by Harry Bishop, one by Jack Thompson—are running dead parallel. Each is on a different tack, heeled over in opposite directions away from each other and headed directly toward the photographer.

With more racing, I learned to *read* the surface of the water, which reveals wind direction and speed to those who learn the technique. This understanding provides a considerable advantage as changes in wind direction and force can often be anticipated. The sails can then be trimmed before the change reaches the sailor. This is particularly important when the wind is light and variable, a common condition on Tippy. Learning and practicing these techniques often makes the difference between first and last in a race.

Over the years, we tried several new types of races. Most lasted but once. We had watermelon races, moonlight races, and several others. One race, the Commodore's Cup, suggested by Al and Norma Hayes in 1986, has become a regular event in mid-July. This race is one heat, the full length of the lake from in front of the dance hall to the flats at the east end and back. I had the pleasure and thrill of winning the first two Commodore's Cup races in my Hobie 16. This occurred during my most successful seasons of racing.

One of the values of being a member of the sailing club was the rehash of the race day with other sailors. We learned so much from each other and especially from those competitors with years of experience. A truly friendly group in spite of being highly competitive, each willingly shared secrets of racing techniques with other members. I learned most of what I know about racing during those meetings or on the water, watching other competitors. I formed numerous friendships among Tippy sailing club members I treasure to this day.

Each season, we held an opening get-together at a member's place, usually in June. For years we had another party during the Fourth of July races. We don't hold the races and the party anymore because of competing activities. Immediately after the Labor Day regatta, we hold our annual meeting, awards dinner and election of officers.

Rod Keesling in the Flying Fish, Bill Christine in his Snipe, and HoJo in his Hobie 16 rounding a mark.

Today, we have two classes racing: monohulls and multihulls or catamarans. Each class uses the Portsmouth handicap system, so all boats compete on an equalized basis. Even inexperienced skippers soon become competitive with the help of our seasoned members. If you have an interest in sailing and good fellowship, come join us. Contact a member or show up at the committee boat—the pontoon flying a colorful windsock at the starting line of the race most Sunday afternoons.

For more information about the sailing club including a schedule of the current season, look up our Web site at clubs.kconline.com/clubs/LTSC.

—*Howard "HoJo" Johnson*, 1998

About the Author (updated in January 2011)

Howard Johnson's first summer on Tippy was 1929 when he was one. His family rented a cottage on Walker's Park. After several summers renting, the Johnson's purchased a lot on Walkers Park and built a cottage there. In 1958, Howard bought the cottage from his dad, also a Howard Johnson, when the senior Johnson built a year-round home on Willow Bend, around the point from the cottage. Howard moved into his mother's house in 1982, several years after his father passed away, to take care of his mother during the summers. In 1985, he became a full-time resident in the house his parents built. In his life, he missed spending summers at Tippy only in 1928 when he was a baby and then in 1952 and 1953 when he lived in California. He now spends winters in St. Augustine, Florida, where he is active in several writers' groups and sings in a local chorus, Singers by the Sea, in Jacksonville Beach.

A Purdue engineer, businessman, and most recently a writer, Howard published his first novel, Blue Shift, in 2002. His novel received a rave review in the Times Union newspaper. Currently, he has several other books in the publishing process, including *Energy, convenient Solutions*, scheduled for release in the summer of 2010. This is a nonfiction book. It describes the many possible and practical ways to solve our energy crisis. Another book, *Memoirs from the Lakeside,* was published late in 2014. An anthology of primarily his memoirs, it also contains some quotes from others. The author describes it as a several decades long *labor of love*. It contains sayings, essays, poems, letters, and short stories, many from his life. He has published several novels including, **The Crystal Feather**, a Sci-Fi story, two thrillers, **Sahm' Allah in St Augustine** and **Days of the High Morning Moon**, and the second novel of the **Blue Shift** trilogy, **Double Jeopardy**.

He also gives talks on several subjects about science, religion, and the environment. One presentation, *Science and Religion: A Reconciliation,* has been constantly updated since its first presentation in 1975. He gives this talk to churches and other groups. Two popular new lectures are about energy and global warming. The one about energy is based on his book, *Energy, Convenient Solutions.* The one about global warming deals with the realities of global warming theories and the current political and media frenzy in a book titled,

Climate and even Worse Dangers We Ignore. This talk and book are described as "a realistic and objective look at the human effects on climate."

Tragically, he lost his wife, Barbara, in 2005 after she fought a losing battle with Post Polio Syndrome. Barbara was a Methodist pastor serving Morris Chapel UMC in Pierceton from 1995 through 2000 when she had to step down because of her illness. He says of Barbara, "She was not only my wife, but my best friend, my proofreader, my editor, and a major contributor and supporter of my writing. Incidentally, she was absolutely brutal with a red pen." There is more about Barbara in several memoirs in my memoir books.

❖ ❖ ❖

If you put the federal government in charge of the Sahara Desert, in 5 years there'd be a shortage of sand.

—*Milton Friedman*

If a child lives with criticism He learns to condemn.
If a child lives with hostility He learns to fight.
If a child lives with ridicule He learns to be shy.
If a child lives with shame He learns to feel guilty.
If a child lives with tolerance He learns to be patient.
If a child lives with praise He learns to appreciate.
If a child lives with fairness He learns justice.
If a child lives with security He learns to have faith.
If a child lives with approval He learns to like himself.
If a child lives with acceptance and friendship
    He learns to find love in the world.

—*Dorothy Law Nolte*

From Consumer Advocate, John Stossel

John Stossel, 20/20 reporter, explains much of what we hear—and what the media say—are myths. In his book, *Myths, Lies, and Downright Stupidity subtitled, Get Out the Shovel Why Everything You Know Is Wrong*, Stossel points out how politicians and activists use anecdotal evidence to prove the truth of concepts factually untrue and often downright harmful. This quote is one of the nearly two-hundred common myths debunked in his book. It is in the chapter about business.

MYTH: Government must make rules to protect us from business.

TRUTH: Competition protects us if government gets out of the way.

It took me a long time to learn that regulations can't protect consumers better than open competition. After all, I worked in newsrooms where *consumer victimization* was a religion and government its messiah. But after fifteen years of watching government regulators make problems worse, I came to understand that we didn't need a battalion of bureaucrats and parasitic lawyers policing business. The competition in the market does that by itself. Word gets out. Angry customers complain to their family and friends; consumer reporters like me blow the whistle on inferior products and shoddy services. Companies with bad reputations lose customers. In a free society, cheaters don't thrive. (At least in business.)

Once I learned more about economics, I saw how foolish I had been. Government uses force to achieve its ends. If you choose not to do what government dictates, men with guns can put you in jail. And clever lawyers will then remove gobs of money from you to get you out. Business, by contrast, cannot use force, no matter how big or powerful they are. So all business transactions are voluntary—no trade is made unless both parties think they benefit. In 1776, economist Adam Smith brilliantly realized that the businessman's self-centered motivation gets strangers to cooperate in producing a multitude of good things: "He intends only his own gain, and he is in this, as in many other cases, led by an invisible hand to promote an end which was no part of his intention".

Few of us appreciate the power of that invisible hand. I don't give my pencil a second thought, and yet I could spend years trying to produce one without turning out anything as *good as the worst pencil available."*

—*John Stossel*

Stossel goes on quoting an essay, *I, Pencil*, by Leonard Read of the Foundation for Economic Education. The essay describes the people equipment and organizations actively involved in gathering the components of the pencil from all over the world. This includes many items: the machines and workers who combine those components, the machines and workers who make those machines, the trucks and ships that carry the raw materiels and finished product around the globe, and the systems that distribute the pencils to the end users. It's an interesting and enlightening bit of prose. I highly recommend reading Stossel's book. It will provide an instructive background for how to accomplish much of what the information contained in these pages describes.

—Howard Johnson, 1998

Human and Simian nature—Hate and destruction - For instinctive reasons, people know it takes far less skill or organization to demolish a home or even the World Trade Center than it does to conceive, design, and build the same thing. Cooperation and creative building are far more demanding, require careful consideration, intelligence, dedication, creative effort and hard work. They are infinitely rewarding and promise a bright and successful future for all, not just the few. This is what we sorely need right now. Unfortunately, conflict is easy. Hate rhetoric and negative campaigning have become so pervasive because their use sways the unthinking masses, mostly the uneducated and poor, those easiest to influence. This is particularly true of the use of class and race hatred. Look at the poor economic results of anger and hatred wherever it surfaces all over the world. Hate is the tool of choice for despots because it is easy. Also, there is a strong sense of human pleasure at seeing those we deem better off than ourselves, damaged, destroyed, or made miserable. It makes no sense, but to the easily led masses, *Getting even* seems preferable to the status quo even when those who do so know they are certain to be rewarded with severe loss, pain, or even death. They become *True Believers* as so well described by Eric Hoffer.

Often attributed to Lincoln in error are these words penned by William J. H. Boetcker, in 1916.

> You cannot strengthen the weak by weakening the strong.
> You cannot help small men by tearing down big men.
> You cannot help the poor by destroying the rich.
> You cannot lift the wage earner by pulling down the wage payer.
> You cannot keep out of trouble by spending more than your income.
> You cannot further the brotherhood of man by inciting class hatreds.
> You cannot establish security on borrowed money.

You cannot build character and courage by taking away a man's initiative and independence.

You cannot help men permanently by doing for them what they could and should do for themselves.

Yet are those not precisely the short lived, instant gratifications politicians and media personalities regularly wield against those they oppose for any reason?

A prediction of where we seem to be headed may have come from far back in history, when the 13 colonies were still part of England. The following quote is often attributed to a Scottish Historian, Alexander Tytler or Tyler. The true origin of the quote is obscure and might have originated in the early 20th century from an unknown politician or writer. Nevertheless, this does not detract from its accuracy.

One version of this quote on why democracies always fail is:

A Democracy cannot exist as a permanent form of government. It can only last until the citizens discover they can vote themselves largesse out of the public treasury. After that, the majority always votes for the candidate promising the most benefits from the public treasury with the result that the Democracy always collapses over a loose fiscal policy, to be followed by a dictatorship, and then a monarchy.

A version of the second part of the misquote, often attributed to Arnold Toynbee is:

The release of initiative and enterprise made possible by self-government ultimately generates disintegrating forces from within. Again and again, after freedom brings opportunity and some degree of plenty, the competent become selfish, luxury-loving and complacent; the incompetent and unfortunate grow envious and covetous, and all three groups turn aside from the hard road of freedom to worship the golden calf of economic security. The historical cycle seems to be: from bondage to spiritual faith; from spiritual faith to courage; from courage to liberty; from liberty to abundance; from abundance to selfishness; from selfishness to apathy; from apathy to dependency, and from dependency back to bondage once more.

But the person who appears to be the actual author of the second part is Henning Webb Prentis, Jr., President of the Armstrong Cork Company. In a speech entitled *Industrial Management in a Republic*, delivered in the grand ballroom of the Waldorf Astoria at New York during the 250th meeting of the National Conference Board on March 18, 1943, and recorded on page 22 of *Industrial Management in a Republic*, Prentis had this to say:

Paradoxically enough, the release of initiative and enterprise made possible by popular self-government ultimately generates disintegrating forces from within. Again and again after freedom has brought opportunity and some degree of plenty, the competent become selfish, luxury-loving and complacent, the incompetent and the unfortunate grow envious and covetous, and all three groups turn aside from the hard road of freedom to worship the Golden Calf of economic security. The historical cycle seems to be: From bondage to spiritual faith; from spiritual faith to courage; from courage to liberty; from liberty to abundance; from abundance to selfishness; from selfishness to apathy; from apathy to dependency; and from dependency back to bondage once more.

At the stage between apathy and dependency, men always turn in fear to economic and political panaceas. New conditions, it is claimed, require new remedies. Under such circumstances, the competent citizen is certainly not a fool if he insists upon using the compass of history when forced to sail uncharted seas. Usually, so-called new remedies are not new at all. Compulsory planned economy, for example, was tried by the Chinese some three millenniums ago, and by the Romans in the early centuries of the Christian era. It was applied in Germany, Italy and Russia long before the present war broke out. Yet it is being seriously advocated today as a solution of our economic problems in the United States. Its proponents confidently assert that government can successfully plan and control all major business activity in the nation, and still not interfere with our political freedom and our hard-won civil and religious liberties. The lessons of history all point in exactly the reverse direction.

These are the real malignancies we must overcome if we are to solve the rapidly growing problems facing not just the US, but the entire world.

It's about time members of groups that constantly denigrate and condemn others out of class or economic envy began to honor and respect the achievements and rewards of those others. I see it as vital we recognize the realities of our situation and the real reasons we are where we are. There has been enough of this debilitating blame game and all of its political distortions and emotional, hate-filled activities. We are engaging in terrible inner political warfare while our enemies stand on the sidelines urging on the various sides and gleefully watching our self destruction.

This is the background of where we are, why we are there, and what we must do to go forward. It has everything to do with what we must overcome in order to counter this growing menace before it destroys us.

—*Howard Johnson - 2003*

Quotes, Letters, Essays, Commentary, and Poetry

Vote early and vote often.   —*Al Capone (1899-1947)*

Memory is the treasury and guardian of all things   —*Cicero, 80 BC*

Power tends to corrupt, and absolute power corrupts absolutely. Great men are almost always bad men.

—*John Emerich Edward Dalberg Acton*

The judgements of men are formed not from facts as they are, but as they wish them to be. They root through tons of good wheat to find three pieces of chaff if the chaff lends weight to their beliefs and argument. It is not that they want others to know the truth, but to have those others believe as they do. Beyond this, they do not care. The conceit of man ordinarily forms his criterion of truth.

—*Unknown*

    There are some who are too proud to yield until compelled by force. They are not to be blamed. It is their privilege; I also, if I think my cause is just, maintain it to the last breath. But let them not blame me when I accept the challenge. I will yield anything for friendship's sake, except a principle that I believe is right.

    As to whether there are gods or not, I am ignorant. I have never set eyes on a god or seen or heard anything, anywhere, that seems to me to justify the belief in gods or to suggest that, if gods there be, their doings justify respect. But I have been observant all my days. Whoever believes there is no such force as destiny directing us and our occasions would waste breath seeking to unconvince me. I have been in the grip of destiny, have seen its shape, have felt the weight of its hand. I know.

—*Lord Tros of Samothrace in* **The Purple Pirate** *by Talbot Mundy*

Our country cannot afford to default on any payments. I pledge to continue to work around Congress and see to it that the debt limit is raised. Where I can act on my own, I'm gonna act on my own. That is leadership.

—*President Barack Hussein Obama*

Obama has some interesting companions who, like him, were nominated for the Nobel peace prize. Among previous nominees are Joseph Stalin and Adolph Hitler.

—*Howard Johnson*

Any form of government is good that actually governs and not offers opportunity to rogues to buy and sell preferment. Let a ruler rule, and let the ruled obey. But woe betide a ruler who is faithless to the lonely task of ruling firmly, justly, decorously, wisely, and to sum the terrifying total . . . well.

I trust or mistrust, having found no middle course worth following. But the charlatan zone between these courses is a wilderness wherein another's treachery by no means can be held to justify my own bad faith. A man must stand or fall, judge and be judged, by his own faith, always.

To an honest man, though I may veil or dissemble my thoughts, I will never leave in doubt the main question: am I for him or against him? Honesty deserves honesty. But I have yet to be persuaded that a lying scoundrel has a claim on me, that I should feel in duty, bound to guide his guessing.

—*Lord Tyros of Samothrace in* **The Purple Pirate** *by Talbot Mundy*

It is enough that the people know there was an election. The people who cast the votes decide nothing. The people who count the votes decide everything.

—*Joseph Stalin*

The fact that we are here today to debate raising America's debt limit is a sign of leadership failure. America has a debt problem and a failure of leadership. Americans deserve better. I, therefore, intend to oppose the effort to increase America's debt.

—*Senator Barack Hussein Obama*

What good fortune for governments that the people do not think. The great strength of the totalitarian state is that it forces those who fear it to imitate it.

—*Adolph Hitler*

There only two possible results when the lion shall lie down with the lamb. The lamb will be eaten, or the lion will starve.

—*Howard Johnson, 2004*

Politics, religion and mob violence have this in common. They are emotional group actions led by messianic control freaks whose only goal is power over easily led groups of people too enthralled and blinded by false rhetoric to think for themselves.

—*Howard Johnson*

Enigma

We place the pieces in the puzzle randomly,
Fitting each together with the one before it.
One doesn't fit. It is taken out,
Turned around. Replaced,
Only to find that it doesn't fit again.
Can the pieces be altered?
Or the puzzle changed?
Or is the only solution in
Putting the pieces into a different maze?

—*Deb Archer to her father, Howard Johnson, 1972*

Epilog to Enigma

The puzzle is nearly complete. The picture almost whole.
    Only a few random spaces remain.
Too many pieces are left over and none of them fit
    And we keep finding more pieces
And more pieces and still more pieces!
    Another puzzle? Another picture?
        More pieces, more puzzles, more pictures!
The puzzles that were wholes
    Become pieces, small random pieces
        That seem to fit still greater puzzles.
We find more puzzles that are pieces
    And few fit . . . and the enigma starts over . . .
        Full cycle . . . at another level . . . ?

—*Reply to "Enigma" sent to Deb Archer by her father, Howard Johnson*

Well-timed silence hath more eloquence than speech.

—*Martin Fraquhar Tupper*

Reflections On and About Columbus Day

Ah, Columbus Day—when Europeans celebrate their discovery of this land. To some of my distant relatives, this is a day of sadness and mourning. A day recognizing a painful turning point in the land where America's original inhabitants lived for hundreds of centuries before the invasion by Europeans. For me, this is a day of mixed emotions. I thank God my Native American blood made peace with my European American blood a long time ago. However, I still get upset when reminded how my European forebears treated my Native American ancestors, particularly the repeatedly violated treaties, but all that is behind us. It's history, and we move forward.

It is time for the forgiving of old injustices and evil acts by long-forgotten ancestors. I firmly object to the recurring demand for reparations for the descendants of slaves. If anyone deserves reparations, it is certainly Native Americans more than and before any other group. I am not in favor of those kinds of reparations either. The time of hatred and recriminations is long gone. It is a time for healing.

Yes, Columbus Day reminds every Native American of repeated raw deals at the hands of Europeans for most of the last five hundred years. Yes, there are frequent grumblings and protest marches on Columbus Day, but they receive little press coverage. In spite of some places where discrimination still exists, most Native Americans now walk proudly as fully accepted members of American society and are proud to be called Americans. They are increasingly returning to their tribal roots for reawakening of their cultural heritage and language. Even more important, the public are now honoring them and their culture as they are increasing numbers of other ethnic, racial, and religious groups. This is a kindly human movement for the most part with expressions in dance, literature, festivals, foods, and song. America's multinational and multi cultural people are more and more honoring their differences, respecting their variety, and enjoying their fellow human beings of all kinds.

Sadly, there are those who never forget and still hold hate in their hearts. Not only do they hold on to hate, but they pass it onto their children and others they can influence. Violent grudges held for centuries and passed down through generations are what make the hells in places like The Middle East, Bosnia, Rwanda, Israel, Afghanistan, and sometimes even New York, Washington, and Pennsylvania. Racial, ethnic, religious, cultural, social, language, political, income, and many other differences can be used to foment hatred, fear, and mob action. This is particularly true among the young or uneducated. Use of these protracted hatreds and twisted religious and political beliefs by unscrupulous leaders to enslave followers is everywhere, including the United States. From small-scale operations like Jim Jones and his cult to David Koresh and the Branch Davidians to some militant blacks and their followers to bin Laden, Al-Qaeda, and all the angry fundamentalists Muslim groups, they have a similar pattern. Adolph Hitler and his Nazis are one monstrous example from the past. Only the scales of death and destruction are different.

The personal question becomes obvious. How do you fight against hatred without using hatred and becoming the very thing you despise? That is a knotty question with few ready or obvious answers. The only real hope is to rally the entire world to help eradicate all manner of hate mongering and the terrorism it fosters wherever it exists. Many members of the media and in political life would do well to curb their own hate speech. They by themselves are not so apt to do direct damage, but there are many among us who become so inflamed by such talk they take actions that are terrorism on whatever scale. The recent, numerous incidents involving Middle Eastern–looking people are examples.

Currently, we are reeling from the results of a major diabolical attack by a group who have been indoctrinated since youth with an unreasoning hatred of our way of life. Make no mistake, groups of evil men are using this calculated and pernicious hatred to gather support for the complete destruction of individual freedoms of all people. They want to impose a false and evilly convoluted version of Islamic law on the entire world by any means possible. Among other things, this law places women in a state worse than slavery. Under their law, these men have the power of life and death over women without question. Women must be completely hidden by clothing and veils when outside. In extreme cases, homes with women must have their windows painted over with black paint or other nonremovable opaque covering so there is no chance of seeing them from outside.

In Afghanistan, the Taliban committed horrible atrocities against women in the name of Islam. Among the worst examples, a group of men dragged a woman out of her car and stoned her to death because she accidentally exposed her arm as she drove. The sports stadium in Kabul was used solely for public executions, usually of women. Many women are killed by their husbands or a relative by having their throat slit with the popular jambiya: a short curved dagger carried by many men.

The following is a quote from a man who spent much of his life in the Middle East and Central Asia. The italics are my words. "These inhuman monsters *by our view* are from a culture that places little value on human life. In the middle east, if you show concern for human life, they conclude that you're a patsy and act accordingly. One example: the Iran hostage affair. They understand murder as we understand humanitarian acts. I don't mean for us to actually commit the murder, but it does deter those people who think you will *commit murder on them*. Then you don't have to do it. Murder is reliable, feasible, and affordable, so the preparations *for war we are now making* send the kind of message that those people understand."

This culture is an extreme example of the cruel subjugation of women by men. It is so radically different from western culture as to be beyond our understanding. It is very much like the cruel male treatment of females found in many troops of baboons. In fact, it probably has the same origins of males so insecure and unable to compete with other males they must take their anger and frustration out on the much weaker females. They do this both individually and in groups because of their inadequacy. It's an example of macho male activity in the extreme.

Recently, my wife, Barbara, and I watched in horror at the TV views of Afghan men beating and executing women in a sports stadium. These so-called Islamic fundamentalists are no more followers of Islam than the average barnyard pig. They are inhuman, satanic monsters—cruel, extreme misogynists who use women as objects for their frustrated hatred and anger. They have been indoctrinated since youth in a satanically twisted version of Islam by teachers whose convoluted, pent-up hate is an expression of their own inadequacy and weakness. The actions of these subhuman creatures display mob mentality of the worst kind. They are in stark contrast to the Muslims who brought forth the light of education, mathematics, astronomy, architecture, and art during the depths of the European Dark Ages. Those great men of knowledge would probably be stoned to death by these slaves of satanic masters if they were around today.

In his book, *The True Believer*, Eric Hoffer describes men who think so little of themselves they can only gain self-esteem by abandoning *self* to a *cause*. These *true believers*, as he calls them, will do anything, including committing suicide, for their cause. Following their *leaders* who enslave them to serve the leader's own and often undefined purpose, these are not men of free will, but true slaves of those who manipulate them. Such are the enemies free men always face.

Man has a natural instinct for enslavement. All movements, large and small, utilize this *pack animal* instinct as tools of opportunistic leaders to control masses of people. Humanitarian civilization tends to counter this instinct while mobs, movements, charismatic leaders, and fundamentalists of many kinds tend to nurture and expand it.

The real power in mobs, movements, fundamentalism, and other uses of instincts to control lies in a simple, irrefutable fact—it is infinitely easier to damage or destroy to change things than to build or create. A few men used only the most rudimentary skills to bring down the World Trade Center in a few hours. Contrast this with the immense time and effort required to design and build those same structures. In the same vein, it is far easier to make angry criticisms of ideas that differ from your own than to listen to those ideas and then make calculated judgments. Closed minds can be true agents of evil.

A simpler illustration, which many have experienced firsthand, is the frequent reaction of small children to sand castles, even those created with hours of careful work. With glee and a real sense of power, a small child will rush through and demolish the creation. It is the rush of power—the instinct for destruction—that creates such childish joy. On any scale, it provides those who feel relatively powerless a form of power over those whom they fear or to whom they feel inadequate for any reason. Vandalism, terrorism, murder, rape—all real crimes—are examples of the destructive efforts of those who feel weak or inadequate in some way directed at those toward whom they feel weakness or inadequacy. Mob action is the lowest form of human expression, but therein lies its power. It is the easiest way for an individual to abandon decency with anonymity and *get back* at real or imagined sources of power.

It will be infinitely more difficult for us to hold our dignity, our respect for all life, our love of freedom, reason, and humanity while engaged in this battle. A battle that is indeed for survival against an enemy that holds an opposite view of almost everything and demands our annihilation in the name of blind subjugation of self to a religion without reason or rationality. Whatever our course, let us pray we do not become like those satanic leaders or their blind followers. Above all, let us take care not to condemn all of Islam and thus fall into the trap these evil men are trying to spring. Islam is not the enemy. The true enemy is ignorance, prejudice, anger, fear, and genuinely evil men who are *true believers* in a twisted fundamentalist Islamic *cause*.

—*Howard Johnson, 1998*

How hard it is to draw the line between a necessary act of justice, and mere malice; between savagery, and proper punishment intended solely to prevent recurrence of something wrong. No matter what the provocation I have found it wiser to abstain from vengeance, but to beware of those upon whom I might have had it. Not always, but not seldom they find it harder to forgive the magnanimity, than it is to forgive their enmity. And it is natural enough: nature is not trusted to direct our motives, only to beglamour them with false names.

—*Talbot Mundy*

All that glitters is not! All's well that ends! A rolling stone gathers! When it rains, it rains!
—*Howard Johnson, 1965*

Smile and the world smiles with you. Cry and your face is a mess.
—*Howard Johnson, 1981*

The Calling

I heard it in fifth grade when my teacher, Mrs. McManus, banished me to the boys' room after I turned in a poem mostly plagiarized. "Howard, you know that is not your poem," she scolded. "Take your notebook and pencil to the boys' room and don't come back until you have written your own poem."

After spending serious effort for two nights, rehashing someone else's work, I put it together as my own poem. Caught in this unforgivable act at such a tender age was a powerful lesson. Alone in the boy's room, I crafted my first real poem in less than half an hour and handed it to my teacher as instructed. It won the award for the fifth grade at Taylor School and was published in the school paper. My family was proud. I never told them the whole story. I first heard the call then but ignored it.

When I was a seventeen-year-old freshman at Purdue, I was placed in a special, advanced creative English course because of the results of my orientation tests. In mid semester, my professor took me aside one day after class to talk about a story I submitted about a boy and his dog.

"You have an unusual talent," he told me. "I knew it when I saw your orientation test results. Your work in this class confirms it. I strongly recommend you switch to journalism."

At that age, I knew that I wanted to be an engineer and ignored his suggestion. Again, I heard the call but ignored it.

While I was in college, I wrote several short stories for an English composition class. That got me going and soon I was writing stories for fun. I remember one story, "A Christmas Tree for Carol," about a blind girl who miraculously recovered her sight when her bed was struck by lightning during a Christmas snow storm. I particularly liked that story and was devastated when my sister told me that it was nonsense because lightning never struck during snow storms. Absolutely certain it did, and yet never having experienced it, I could call on no personal knowledge. A few years later, I was standing by the back door of my wife's parents' home in a blinding snow storm before Christmas when a brilliant flash lit up the whole sky. The loud thunder that followed confirmed it was lightning. As I stood there watching flash after flash, I remembered that story and my sister's words. I was vindicated. I have since learned thunder snow storms are not terribly rare. Again the urge to write came over me, and I wrote several stories that Christmas season. Yet again, I ignored the call.

As the years went by, I collected quotes, witticisms, and poetry I liked. Occasionally I would write an essay, poem, or short story. Each time, I would wonder if I could write something of value. During the seventies, my daughter Deb sent me a poem she wrote entitled, "Enigma." I immediately answered her with my own poem, "Epilog to Enigma." Those two poems remain among my favorites. This experience triggered a short flurry of writing which included one wild poem titled, "Sound Rainbow." My poem won an award and was published in a collection of poetry in 2000. This time the call held me for a while, but once more I turned and ignored it.

In 1981, I spent nearly a year working in the Philippines. While there, I began writing descriptive letters and experimenting with haiku, a highly condensed Japanese form of poetry that uses few words to paint a picture. It was at this time the first ideas for a novel began going through my head when going off to sleep. I tried various ideas to start weaving into a novel. Though I heard the call quite loudly then, I still ignored it.

In 1984, I bought my first computer, an IBM XT clone made by Zenith. I used it with AutoCAD software as a design tool for the dental offices I was designing for a living. It was much quicker and easier than the paper and ink I had been using. In the software I received with the system was a word processor named Word Perfect. It wasn't long before I began using Word Perfect to write stories, essays, and poetry. Several times I even began the novel I dreamed about. Still, my main effort was not in that direction. I heard the call once more but still did not listen.

Soon I was all wrapped up in a struggling computer business I started with hardly a nickel to my name. Survival was the name of the game, and all my efforts were so aimed. In 1990, I met a lovely little lady who soon became the focus of my life. Both of us were soon singing in the choir of the little Methodist Church in Leesburg. On friendship Sunday in October of 1992, I stood up in the choir loft during our sharing of joys and concerns and proposed. Incredibly, one of our members was videotaping the service, so we have a complete record of the proposal and Barbara's acceptance on tape. The following May, we were married in the same church. I continued with the computer business while Barbara became a Methodist minister and was appointed to a nearby small country church. The call kept getting louder and more persistent.

In 1999, I started writing my long-considered novel in earnest. Working from five in the morning until about nine or ten, I wrote feverishly. Those four or five hours each morning flew by as the story miraculously appeared on the computer screen before my eyes. It became much more like reading a novel than writing. New characters and circumstances appeared out of nowhere as my main characters became real people to me experiencing real-life situations. Never in my life have I enjoyed doing anything more. Well into the story, I realized one book could not tell the entire story, so I decided to make it into a trilogy. This time I heard the call loud and clear and I answered. I was hooked. Writing soon became my main passion in life.

It took eight months to write the first book and fourteen more months to rewrite it. About the time I finished the first draft, I found and joined an international group of writers named Science Fiction Novelists who critique each other's work. This wonderful group of writers, from all walks of life, provided invaluable assistance in the rewriting of my book. Without their excellent (and sometimes brutal) critiques, my rewrite would not have gone nearly so well. I was so encouraged with my writing that I sold the PC business in June of 2000 to pursue a writing career full-time. We decided that with Barb's salary as a pastor and my social security, we could survive until my writing began to pay off.

Then misfortune struck as Barbara's health suddenly began to deteriorate. Soon after I sold the business and after nearly six years spent in the pulpit, she was incapacitated by the pain and weakness of post polio syndrome. On December 31, 2000, she stepped down from the pulpit. It was the saddest day of our lives together. Not too long after this emotionally draining and terribly devastating event, she began helping me by proofing my writing. Soon she was my invaluable aid in editing, proofing, and rewriting my work. Her expertise in English and totally different nontechnical view of the world from my own, became an essential factor in my work. Without it, my writing would not be nearly as readable or grammatically correct. In short, we became a writing team.

On January 8, 2002, I composed and sent the following letter:

To my treasured family and friends:

I do believe I have discovered who and what I am.

This Christmas, my daughter Debby gave me a book entitled *For Writers Only* by Sophy Burnham. I opened it immediately and read these words by the author, "I give this book then to all writers, to all creative people, to all of us poor troubled humans who are struggling with our doubts and love. I hope that it will live in your hands until it drops, stained and dog-eared, into dust, too yellowed and frayed even for the outdoor racks of second-hand bookstores. I hope you steal it from libraries and buy it in stores to give to your sons or wives or daughters or nephews or husbands or mothers, in order to encourage them to write the stories of their hearts.

"For we all have stories. And they must be told. In telling our stories, we affirm ourselves, our being, and thereby the purpose of our creator and our lives."

This book's cover says, "Inspiring thoughts on the exquisite pain and heady joy of the writing life, from its great practitioners."

A quick glance through the first few pages fulfilled the promise of marvelous thoughts from kindred souls. If ever I knew who and what I am, I do now. This book reached my soul and prompted me to say, "I am a writer." In one of the early pages, a John Gardner quote said, "True artists, whatever smiling faces they may show you, are obsessive, driven people." As I search for more quotes to share, I realize all these writers say what I so deeply feel. Each quoted paragraph is a footnote to the man I found myself to be. However, there is one repeated comment that misses me completely. Several writers describe the pain of the empty void that comes when a work is finished, the empty mind searching for a new verbal mission. I have never experienced that emptiness.

In fact, I know I will not live long enough to empty my thoughts of valid things to put to paper. Writing my first novel was an unbelievable joy. I hated even those interruptions for biological necessities such as food, sleep, and others. Typically, I wrote during the silence of the morning from five until nine or ten. It took eight months of every moment I could spare to complete the book. Then it took another fourteen months of equal dedication for me to rewrite it. Even that was a great joy as I carefully read and re crafted phrase after phrase and paragraph after paragraph. Robert Heinlein said in one of his books on writing that a novelist was a true storyteller who read more than wrote his story. I found that to be quite true. In fact, it was an unbelievable joy to write a story that created itself as it went along. New situations, new characters, and new actions constantly appeared spontaneously as the words seemed to place themselves on the screen. Although I certainly had a rough idea of the story, the details seemed to come from nowhere, like an actual happening. This never ceased to amaze me.

When a day starts as I sit in front of that magic screen, I am never sure what is going to happen, or even what I am about to write for that matter. After finishing *Blue Shift*, I started immediately on the second book of the trilogy. A third completed, that book now waits as I struggle to work other more pressing thoughts into organized words. During the last six months, I have completed a collection of quotes, poems, comments, and short stories into a book entitled *Words from the Lakeside* as well as two collections of essays, *Thoughts on the Cultures of Today* and *The Feudals*. The first collection contains a number of essays about things we don't often think about yet which profoundly affect our lives. My book, *The Feudals*, is a collection of essays and comments about the intellectual elite who control the media and much of the extreme political left. I call them Feudals after the political system of the Middle Ages to which they seem so bent on reviving. These books are not politically correct. I have tried to write with frankness. As a result, I have doubtless written something in each of them that will please or compliment as well as offend or insult each reader. That was done incidently, not intentionally. I call myself an equal opportunity pleaser/offender.

More recently I have been writing memoirs, mostly putting on record stories of my life which I have told and retold over the years, or which have particularly strong memories. I started out with a list of eight. By the time I had written four of those, the list had grown to twenty-five. The writing of a true story requires details which, when dredged up from deep in memory, bring to mind other memories that need to be told. My excitement continues to grow almost exponentially. To paraphrase—so many stories, so little time. Like the proverbial kid in the candy store, I hardly know where to start.

As a seventeen-year-old student in an advanced composition course in my freshman year of college, I was told I had the tools to be an effective writer. My professor urged me to transfer from engineering to journalism. My mind and heart were set on becoming an engineer, so I didn't listen then. Now, his words reverberate in my head. I have no regrets for my choice, for I have had an exciting, event-filled life of many joys and marvelous experiences with friends and an incredible family. Now, in my seventies, I am truly a writer. It's all I want to do. I think, or at least hope, I am good at it, and perhaps time and good fortune will now smile on me once more. Each moment stolen from writing hurts somehow. There is never enough time to say what must be said. Each word I read written by others demands a thousand in reply. I could not possibly live long enough to say what I must say.

Even if I never sell another book, article, story, or poem, I will still be pleased with what I have done. I have two closing quotes:

To believe your own thoughts, to believe that what is true for you in your private heart is true for all men—that is genius.

—*Ralph Waldo Emerson*

The world has no room for cowards. We must all be ready somehow to toil, to suffer, to die. And yours is not less noble because no drum beats before you when you go out to your daily battlefields, and no crowds shout your coming when you return from your daily victory and defeat.

—*Robert Louis Stevenson*

Love to you all, Howard Johnson - January 8, 2002

February 4, 2002: At this point in time, my first novel, *Blue Shift*, is about to be released. I am well into the writing of the second book of the proposed trilogy which I am hopeful will be completed within the year. I am currently putting the finishing touches on several other books, mostly nonfiction, including; *Words from the Lakeside*, a collection of quotes, comments, poems, short stories, and other writings; *Images of Pain*, comments and responses, mostly e-mail, triggered by the September 11 attack; *Thoughts on the Cultures of Today*, essays about many of the problems now facing humanity; *The Feudals*, political commentary and opinions about the challenges facing Americans. As these words are written, Barbara and I are traveling westward from Texas through New Mexico on our way to Arizona and California. I set up my laptop at each motel and work on my short stories each morning until Barbara wakes up. Even as I write, the adventures continue.

July 8, 2002: Much has happened since the last chapter. Early in February, we arrived in Visalia, California, to visit my daughter Deborah and her husband, Michael. Barbara's hands and feet were becoming more paralyzed every day as her condition steadily worsened. Thanks to the suggestion of a doctor friend of my daughters' I took Barbara to the Sansum Clinic in Santa Barbara. After emergency spinal surgery, a heart attack, and twelve weeks in a halo device, Barb was much better than she was before we left home in January and was improving each week. While here, my book came out, and we received five hundred copies that now reside in Deb and Michael's garage. After calling on bookstores in Visalia and Fresno, I held my first signing at the Magic Dragon bookstore in Visalia. There, I sold and signed eleven books. It was an exciting learning experience, not terribly successful, but certainly not a failure.

July 21, 2002: Home at last. We arrived precisely six months to the day we left home. This is an ongoing tale. While I may add to it from time to time, someone else will have to write the final paragraphs.

January 26, 2007: Since my last entry, my life has been turned upside down and inside out. I lost my precious Barbara on October 16, 2005, after a long steady decline in her health and ability to get around. During this period, I shelved my writing except for a few essays and short stories. I have also written a lot more about Barbara in several memoirs and essays in my books of memoirs. After a period of recovery and adjustment to life alone, I have returned to completing the book, *Words from the Lakeside*, and have finished another, a nonfiction study of our energy crisis and what to do about it titled *A Convenient Solutions*. It is my hope that both books will be published by the end of next year.

As I again look toward restarting to work on the *Blue Shift* series and several other novels, I find myself with a new lady in my life, Daphne. We are both in a period of readjustment in our lives, having each lost a dearly beloved spouse. Who knows what the future holds for us, but for now, we are adjusting and enjoying being together, one day at a time. Each day a bonus is how we look at the future.

January 18, 2009: Finally, my book on energy, *A Convenient Solution*, is about to be released, almost two years after I thought it would be. If I had ever known how much work it was going to take to get this book into print, I might never have started. Believe me, fiction is far easier to write for many reasons. I had to rewrite virtually every page of this book several times—some dozens of times. Confirming research reports with multiple sources and then recognizing the differences between opinions and facts took a Great deal of effort and great gobs of time. Thanks to Daphne's efforts for the last two years, I have softened my expressions in the book of many of my positions on debatable subjects, primarily political. Unfortunately, even being neutral on some subjects can rile some people. For example, I am quite neutral about global warming. I do not think it is a serious or human caused problem, but only because the current science on the subject is quite flimsy, ambiguous, and inadequate. Show me some definitive and conclusive data confirming human caused global warming and I'll get on the bandwagon. Until such time, I stay neutral, being neither a subjective supporter nor denier.

I've published my first book of memoirs, **Memoirs from the Lakeside** and am well into writing a second one, **Words from the Lakeside**. I have several new novels in progress, Blue Shift III, and an unnamed semi-historical novel involving native Americans. Writing these novels is a great deal more fun than writing non fiction. 'Nuff said!

September 22, 2009: I find it hard to believe that I am still working on my book on energy, *A Convenient Solution*. I keep finding reasons to make minor changes both to correct small errors and to respond to suggestions about layout or content from people whose opinions I trust. Also, new, important information about energy is constantly coming to my attention. Information that simply must be added to the content. Numerous Internet links and references must be removed as they are no longer available. While I decry the continuing delays in publication, I am thankful these changes and corrections are being made **before** the book is released. As these words are being written, the final galleys of the book are being sent electronically to my publisher. The first copies of the book should now be available in October, probably while we are away on a major trip.

My book, *Memoirs from the Lakeside*, is also in the final edit process and might even be available before the others, something I never thought possible. I have discovered how much work must go into finishing a book and making it ready for publication, especially when the author must rely on friends and his own effort to supply the necessary finishing touches.

Though the promotion of these books will consume much of my time for the rest of the year and well into next year, I can hardly wait to get back to work on several writing projects that were set aside, so these two books could be finished. From now on I will stick to fiction and try to complete these five other projects. They are in various stages from beginning to about 60% completed. How much easier it is to conceive of a new project than to complete one already started. I have made a promise to myself not to start another one until at least two of the ones I have already started are either finished or abandoned as not being worthy of the effort.

July 27, 2010: Will my book on energy ever be released? After an unbelievable software glitch that has cost me quite a bit of money and a lot of valuable time, my final files are once more off to the printer. I still have 450 of the original books in boxes in the garage. They have such egregious errors they cannot even be used for promotion. Nearly a hundred errors had to be carefully found and corrected, errors caused by an errant word processor whose developer says what happened was impossible. When I sent them a copy of the file with the errors, they quit talking to me and wouldn't answer my calls. Thank you Corel.

With Word Perfect continuing to generate errors on its own, I had to develop my own system for creating errorless Adobe Acrobat pdf files. It was a lot of work and delayed the release for at least three months. To make certain there was no confusion, I renamed the book, *Energy, Convenient Solutions*. I also rewrote a number of sections because of new information. I have checked each of the 280 pages in the final pdf file for errors. Although I probably missed a few, it's going to press as it is. The new name is far more search-engine friendly than *A Convenient Solution*, a big deal in the age of rapidly growing Internet commerce.

December 10, 2010: *Energy, Convenient Solutions* is finished and available in hardcover, paperback, and ebook through most popular book outlets. My book pof memoirs, *Memoirs from the Lakeside*, has been approved for publication and will be hopefully be available in 2011.

For my birthday in 2011 my thoughtful Daphne gave me a canvas bag with the following appropriate quotes:

"The only end to writing is to enable the readers better to enjoy life, or better to endure it."
—Samuel Johnson - 1709 - 1781

"When the itch of literature comes over a man, nothing can cure it but the scratching of a pen."
—Samuel Lover - 1797 - 1868

November 26, 2012: (my 85th birthday) I have been quite busy since my last entry in this blog. Some two dozen articles I wrote about energy and my book, *Energy, Convenient Solutions*, have been published in trade and local magazines. The Tucson Citizen, the only sizeable newspaper to review my book, published a glowing review. I couldn't have done better if I wrote it myself.

This edition of my anthology/collection, *Words from the Lakeside*, has been published replacing the first edition which is no longer available. The explanation of the changes from the original is on page 1. The SciFi short stories were combined with an equal number of new short stories. The resulting collection is was released early in 2012. *Starring*, is the name I gave this collection of short stories, most of which are SciFi. I have D. Keith Howington, a member of my Science Fiction Novelists critique group to thank for that name which I like. Everything escept the short stories that were in the original *Words from the Lakeside*, have been combined with many new memoirs and is titled, *Memoirs from the Lakeside*. In this book, I share a number of interesting and often exciting life experiences from my long and active life. It too was released in 2012.

I also have two non fiction projects nearing completion. One is a collection of political essays titled, *The Feudals*. (Those on the far left and far right would probably call it fiction) The other is a collection of essays about possible solutions to many of our painful problems titled simply, *Solutions*. The first is nearing completion while the second is at least a year away from publication.

The Crystal Feather, a very different kind of SciFi novel was released in 2012. I am proud to announce that *The Crystal Feather*, though unfinished at the time, won first place in the Florida Writers Association Lighthouse novel contest of nearly 400 entries. Required entry was the first two chapters and a synopsis of the rest. Work on my energy book delayed the completion of my other projects more than I liked. Once it was released I returned to my first love, fiction. Hopefully I can now get down to business finishing the projects I have started.

I currently have four novel projects underway, Three are SciFi including *Blue Shift II and III* which are each about half completed. *Carol Hughes*, a distinctly different SciFi novel, is about a third completed. I am also working on a historical novel about native Americans (some of my forebears) from the late 1700's up to today. In this story, I plan to use some of my grandfather's tales about our Indian ancestors. I hope I live long enough to complete these projects and even others already coursing through my head.

In October 2011, I started what for me is an entirely different type of novel, a suspense thriller. The name of this novel is *Days of the High Morning Moon*. It has become a welcome diversion from writing memoirs or Sci-Fi, my usual venues. It was finished and published in 2015 and is now available on Amazon and Senesis Word. It has already broadened my writing skills. Writing this has also inspired me to finish the Sci-Fi novels I have already started. Whenever I get stuck (writer's block) on whichever of those I happen to be writing, I switch over to another project and that clears my mind. When I go back to my Sci-Fi novels, the block is almost always gone.

✷ ✷ ✷

When you do the common things in life in an uncommon way, you will command the attention of the world.

—*George Washington Carver (1864-1943)*

Images of Pain

A Satanic burst of flame - Screaming, burning flesh - Bright tinkling shards of glass - Another monstrous flash of fire - Black smoke billowing - Heart-rending phone calls - Humanity in the stairwells - Electronic pictures burned into brains - A rumbling, crushing, obliterating collapse - Terrible showers of stone, steel, glass, dust, and flesh - Lives painfully obliterated as millions watch in horror and disbelief - Booming clouds of smoke and dust, then dooming silence.

Heroic thousands in vain efforts - Photos of lost loved ones - Withering hope - Veils of tears - Anguish a billionfold, but a few scream with joy - Faces of horrible pain of loss - Electronic images of child faces of evil - I cry, you cry, millions cry, God cries. Satan laughs!

—*Howard Johnson, September 11, 2001*

In any so-called *equal* society, there will always be those who are more *equal* than others.
—the words of George Orwell in **Animal Farm** as adapted by Howard Johnson, 2001

"If you can't say somethin' nice, don't say nothin' at all!
—*Thumper in Bambi, Quoted by Howard Johnson November 2001*

Liberalism is a serious mental disorder.

—*Jules P. Guidry, 2012*

>One midnight, deep in starlight still,
>I dreamed that I received this bill:
>   (-------- in account with life:)
>Five thousand breathless dawns, all new;
>Five thousand flowers, fresh with dew;
>Five thousand sunsets, wrapped in gold;
>One million snowflakes, served ice-cold;
>Five quiet friends; a baby's love;
>One white-mad sea, with clouds above;
>One hundred music-haunted dreams
>Of moon-drenched roads and hurrying streams;
>Of prophesying winds, and trees;
>Of silent stars and browsing bees;
>One June night in a fragrant wood;
>One heart that loved and understood.
>I wondered when I waked at day,
>How . . . how in God's name
>   . . . I could pay!

—*Courtland Sayers*

To accuse others for one's own misfortunes is a sign of want of education. To accuse oneself shows that one's education has begun. To accuse neither oneself nor others shows that one's education is complete.

—*Epictetus (55-135 A.D.*

O suns and skies and clouds of June,
And flowers of June together,
Ye cannot rival for one hour
October's bright blue weather;

When loud the bumblebee makes haste,
Belated, thriftless vagrant,
And goldenrod is dying fast,
And lanes with grapes are fragrant;

When gentians roll their fingers tight
To save them for the morning,
And chestnuts fall from satin burrs
Without a sound of warning;

When on the ground red apples lie
In piles like jewels shining,
And redder still on old stone walls
Are leaves of woodbine twining;

When all the lovely wayside things
Their white-winged seeds are sowing,
And in the fields still green and fair,
Late aftermaths are growing;

When springs run low, and on the brooks,
In idle golden freighting,
Bright leaves sink noiseless in the hush
Of woods, for winter waiting;

When comrades seek sweet country haunts,
By twos and twos together,
And count like misers, hour by hour,
October's bright blue weather.

O sun and skies and flowers of June,
Count all your boasts together,
Love loveth best of all the year
October's bright blue weather.

> This was one of my dad's favorite poems. He repeated the first four lines to me many times, especially in October at the lake. I always had it in my mind that it was written by James Whitcomb Riley, but researching it to put in my book I discovered the actual author. She wasn't even a Hoosier. Helen Hunt Jackson was born in Amherst Massachusetts and lived much of her life in Colorado Springs and southern California. A fiery and prolific writer, Jackson engaged in heated exchanges with federal officials over the injustices committed against American Indians. Several of her books reflected her efforts supporting Indian causes. Her novel *Ramona* was a very popular book about the troubles of an Indian family. Details of her life and writing can be found on the Internet at:
>
> **http://en.wikipedia.org/wiki/Helen_Hunt_Jackson**

—*Helen Hunt Jackson (1830-1885)*

Honest work bears a lovely face, for it is the father of pleasure and the mother of good fortune. It is the keystone of prosperity and the sire of fame. And best of all, work is relief from sorrow and the handmaiden of happiness.

—Unknown

Indeed . . . Man does not live by bread alone,
    but without bread, man does not live at all!

—Howard Johnson, 1983

Socialism has a record of failure so blatant that only an intellectual could ignore or evade it

—Thomas Sowell.

Love is friendship set on fire.

—Jeremy Taylor

Heavens! How many obstacles there are between a resolution and its fulfillment! How much compromising to be done with unessential issues to preserve the main thing whole and worthy! Each new obstacle to be surmounted in its turn, its smashed entanglements converted into means toward the main end! And the main end never to be overlooked, forgotten, substituted, changed, abandoned, nor once dishonored by a coward doubt! The worst hour is the eve of the final effort, when the goal that seemed so near, seems passing out of reach, and all the work done hitherto that seemed so wise, appears ill done and ill-conceived, and all the unpredictable, imponderable dangers suddenly invade the mind like specters. Then a man needs courage. Aye, he needs the courage to believe his vision all along, from the first until now, was clear, and all his efforts well aimed to a good conclusion.

—Talbot Mundy in Tros of Samothrace

In human intercourse the tragedy begins, not when there is a misunderstanding about words, but when silence is not understood.

—Henry David Thoreau

By doubting we are led to inquire;
    by inquiring we perceive the truth.

—Peter Abelard

The most fundamental fact about the ideas of the political left is that they do not work. Therefore we should not be surprised to find the left concentrated in institutions where ideas do not have to work in order to survive.

—*Thomas Sowell*

Slow me down, Lord!
Ease the pounding of my heart by the quieting of my mind.
Steady my hurried pace with a vision of the eternal reach of time.
Give me, amidst the confusion of the day, the calmness of the everlasting hills.
Break the tension of my nerves with the soothing music of the singing streams that live
    in my memory.
Help me to know the magical restoring power of sleep.
Teach me the art of taking minute vacations of slowing down;
To look at a flower; To chat with an old friend or make a new one;
To pat a stray dog; To watch a spider build a web;
To smile at a child; To read from a good book.
Remind me each day that the race is not always to the swift;
That there is more to life than increasing speed.
Let me look upward into the towering oak and know that it grows
great and strong because it grew slowly and well.

—*Orin L. Crain*

Choose, and take the consequences. Choose to command, and learn the pain of the barbed treachery of envy. Choose to obey, and learn how soon obedience begets contempt. Choose the philosopher's life, and learn the famished waste of thought that, like a barren woman, lusts unpregnant. Choose . . . or become the victim of others' choosing.

—*Talbot Mundy in* Tros of Samothrace

Tradition means giving votes to the most obscure of all classes, our ancestors. It is the democracy of the dead.

—*G. K. Chesterton*

The problem with socialism is that eventually you run out of other people's money.

—*Margaret Thatcher*

The greatest test of courage on the earth is to bear defeat without losing heart.

—*Robert G. Ingersoll, 1833–1899*

If you give a man a fish, he has food for a day.
If you teach him to fish, he has food from then on.
—*Chinese Proverb*

If you give a man a fish, he has food for a day.
If you teach him to fish, he will sit in a boat all day and drink beer.
—*Unknown*

The best argument for Christianity is Christians: their joy, their certainty, their completeness.

But the strongest argument against Christianity is also Christians: when they are somber and joyless, when they are self-righteous and smug, when they are narrow and repressive, then Christianity dies a thousand deaths.
—*From a sermon by Pastor Barbara Johnson quoted from Sheldon Vanauken, April 1997*

If you can start the day without caffeine or pep pills,
If you can be cheerful, ignoring aches and pains,
If you can resist complaining and boring people with your troubles,
If you can eat the same food every day and be grateful for it,
If you can understand when loved ones are too busy to give you time,
If you can overlook when people take things out on you when, through
    no fault of yours, something goes wrong,
If you can take criticism and blame without resentment,
If you can face the world without lies and deceit,
If you can conquer tension without medical help,
If you can relax without liquor,
If you can sleep without the aid of drugs,
Then . . . You're actually a dog.
—*E-mail from Brenda Shears to Nancy Grimm, October 30, 2001*

To be a friend a man should not attempt to reform or reprimand, but should strive only to make others happy if he can.
—*Wilfred A. Peterson*

Logic is in the eye of the logician.
—*Gloria Steinem*

Heroes and Oracles, Where Have They Gone?

Emerson remarked, "Each man is a *hero* and an *oracle* to somebody."

Noah Webster describes a *hero* as "a prominent or central personage taking an admirable part in any remarkable action or event; as the *hero* of a romance; hence, a person regarded as a model of noble qualities; as, Washington is more than a national *hero*."

He describes an *oracle* as "the medium by which God reveals hidden knowledge or makes known the Devine purpose; also, the place where the oracle is given."

Like it or not, we all have heroes and oracles who we use to shape our actions, character, and beliefs. They are the winds that bend the twig into the tree.

Pick carefully your heroes for as they are, so will you become!
—Howard Johnson, 1998

On Idealism

To be idealistic and naive is to lay oneself open to charlatans and con men of all types. To discard naivete only stops the most obvious of these, and at what price?

To discard idealism in order to keep oneself safe from frauds and connivers creates total constipation of the soul, a deplorable condition.

I believe it is best to be idealistic and naive, but secure wise counsel before making life-changing decisions. Ah, but securing wise counsel, there's the rub. A quote from Talbot Mundy: "When a number of men, for a number of different reasons, counsel me to turn aside from danger, I have usually found it wise to recognize the danger, but do the opposite of what they urge. Although they likely know it not, their counsel is directed either by their own necessity or by their love of comfort, good repute and profit."

If you remain true to your idealism, you will surely be duped on occasion. But if losses are kept small while ideals and naivete are held, you will be able to smile at life and have numerous dear friends. Or perhaps, you search for something else?

—Howard Johnson, May 25, 2001

I will stand with the Muslims should the political winds shift in an ugly direction.
—*from: Audacity of Hope - Barack Hussein Obama*

Light appears in the darkness . . . a filmy, tenuous, reaching thing that invades the being that is the searcher. This delicious, tantalizing something, like the aroma of fresh food to a starving creature, draws the searcher inexorably onward. First, an awareness like the quick surge of the stag's head to an unfamiliar scent as he chooses between fear-driven flight and the search for knowing.

Light draws, destroying the nothing darkness, gradually tapping the entire concentration of the searcher until a delay of the blink of the eye becomes an agonizing pain of loss. Drawn as the ancient seamen to the sirens, the searcher bends his entire being toward the light. He must know . . . is it merely a firefly or perhaps a star?
—*Howard Johnson, 1970*

Thought for the day: In today's topsy-turvy world, it is **not** okay to call a person a slut or whoremonger, but it **is** okay to be one!
—*Howard Johnson, 1999*

Faith without credulity, Conviction without bigotry, Charity without condescension, Courage without pugnacity, Self-respect without vanity, Humility without obsequiousness, Love of humanity without sentimentality, Meekness with power.
—*Charles Evans Hughes, 1862–1948*

To bear up under loss;
To fight the bitterness of defeat and the weakness of grief;
To be victor over anger;
To smile when tears are close;
To resist disease and evil men and base instincts;
To hate hate and love love;
To go on when it would seem good to die;
To look up with unquenchable faith in something ever more to be.
That is what any man can do, and be great.

—*Zane Grey*

Mr. Wagner has beautiful moments but bad quarters of an hour.
—*Gioacchino Rossini (1792-1868)*

In children we have an innocent audience not yet hardened and brutalized and made cynical. They look to us trustingly for information and enchantment. How very few of us are worthy of such trust.

—*Sterling North*

>He who knows nothing, loves nothing.
>He who can do nothing, understands nothing.
>He who understands nothing is worthless.
>But, he who understands also loves, notices, sees . . .
>The more knowledge is inherent in a thing, the greater the love.
>Anyone who imagines that all fruits ripen at the same time as strawberries, knows nothing about grapes.

—*Paracelsus*

Of all Life's difficulties, I have found it hardest to compel myself to recognize and concede a woman's right to meet me on even terms. But it seems equally hard for a woman to understand my attitude. No more than all the priests, philosophers and poets do I know what love is. Unlike many of them, I am unwilling to pretend that I do know. Neither do I know what life is. But it seems to me that if love or life lack dignity, neither the one nor the other is worth the sacrifice of half a moment's thought.

—*Talbot Mundy in* Purple Pirate

The desire to transcend the human condition is an invitation to tyranny.

—*Gertrude Himmelfarb*

Add a few drops of venom to a half truth and you have an absolute truth.

—*Eric Hoffer*

Everything has been figured out, except how to live.

—*Jean-Paul Sartre (1905-1980)*

No one can earn a million dollars honestly.

—*William Jennings Bryan (1860-1925)*

One Man's Opinion on Being a Christian

To follow the teachings of Jesus does not mean putting on the trappings of a Christian to show others. Nor does it demand that others practice Christianity the same way we do. Jesus never forced a single person to follow him. He left that choice up to us. He never demanded we look like him, dress like him, speak the same language as him, eat the same food as him, or bow down and worship him!

He never had a church or a parish. He asked only that we believe in him as the son of God and let our hearts follow his. As a boy of twelve, he questioned the priests in the synagogue. Should we not then, in following his example, question authorities of the church, if only to keep them on their toes?

Was not "Go now and sin no more!" his only command after forgiving? How about "Let he who is without sin cast the first stone!"

Is not this a charge for us to refrain from condemning others in our own lives? In washing the feet of the disciples at the Last Supper, did he not demonstrate the ultimate equality of the leader as a servant to those he leads?

Jesus showed us that by answering to ourselves in understanding, we would be serving him. Being a Christian is not a goal to be reached but a searching and striving within each Christian to be more *Christlike* each day of our lives—a private, personal drive within our hearts and souls. To be a Christian is always to lead by example as he did.

—Howard Johnson, March 14, 1999

Enlightened people seldom or never possess a sense of responsibility

—George Orwell

True value in life lies not in finding that which we like, but in liking what we find. The secret of happiness is not in doing that which we like, but in liking that which we must do.

—Howard Johnson, December 1980

Every former protester I know passionately defends the actions of the 1960s and early '70s as exercising our First-Amendment right to criticize government policies. None seems to have read the First Amendment to the end where it speaks about peaceably to assemble, and to petition the government. More importantly, even in their advanced years, many seem incapable to confront the reality of having served the interest of America's enemies.

—*Balint Vazsonyi*

The Bridge Builder

An old man, going a lone highway,
    Came, at evening, cold and gray,
To a chasm, vast and deep and wide,
    Through which was flowing a sullen tide.
The old man crossed in the twilight dim:
    The sullen stream had no fears for him.
But he turned, when safe on the other side.
    And built a bridge to span the tide.
"Old man," said a fellow pilgrim, near,
    "You are wasting strength with building here;
Your journey will end with the ending day;
    You never again must pass this way;
You have crossed the chasm deep and wide,
    Why build you the bridge at eventide?"
The builder lifted his old gray head:
    "Good friend, in the path that I have come," he said,
"There followeth after me today
    A youth, whose feet must pass this way.
This chasm, that has been naught to me
    To that fair-haired youth may a pitfall be.
He, too, must cross in the twilight dim;
    Good friend, I am building the bridge for him."

—*Will Allen Dromgoole*

More tears are shed over answered prayers than unanswered ones.

—Saint. Teresa of Avila

If there were no God, there would be no atheists.

—G. K. Chesterton

As for me, I am a mystic, not denying what I merely do not like or do not understand, nor claiming absoluteness for the truth I think I know. And I believe, and enjoy believing, that a greater mystery than human mind can know, selects and sets us amid flames of love and hate, wherein we forge new weapons and for them new uses, and for our souls new destiny.

—Talbot Mundy in Purple Pirate

God sends children for another purpose
    than merely to keep up the race;
To enlarge our hearts, and to make us unselfish
    and full of kindly sympathies and affections;
To give our souls higher aims;
To call out all our facilities to extended enterprise and exertion;
And to bring round our firesides bright faces,
    happy smiles and tender hearts.

—Mary Howitt, 1799–1888

A trained flea can be taught to do most the things a congressman does.

—Mark Twain

He who has begun, has the work half done.

—Horace, 65–8 BC

Is the music a tool of the performer?
    Or is the performer a tool of the music?
Is the message the tool of the author?
    Or is the author a tool of the message?

—Howard Johnson, 2001

People unfit for freedom—who cannot do much with it—are hungry for power. The desire for freedom is an attribute of a *have* type of self. It says: leave me alone and I shall grow, learn, and realize my capacities. The desire for power is basically an attribute of a *have not* type of self.

—*Eric Hoffer*

Beauty of face and body attracts only; it cannot hold, nor will it last for long. Beauty of heart, on the other hand, grows with time, holds people together, and brings joy to all who have the good fortune to share it. Ah! But beauty of soul, the greatest of all, makes life worth living for everyone touched by it, whether for a brief moment or a lifetime.

—*Howard Johnson, 1974*

Another New Serenity Prayer

May God, the order of the universe,
> grant me the serenity to understand belief,

The courage to accept truth,
> and the wisdom to know the difference.

—*Howard Johnson, February 20, 2001*

It is best to be careful what family you choose to be born into!

—*Howard Johnson, January 1999*

Oh what a tangled web we weave when first we practice to deceive!

—*Sir Walter Scott, 1771–1832*

To which J. R. Pope replied:

But when we've practiced quite a while how vastly we improve our style.

—*J. R. Pope, 1874–1937*

Bigamy is having one wife/husband too many. Monogamy is the same.

—*Oscar Wilde*

The superior man is modest in his speech, but exceeds in his actions.

—*Confucius*

To reach another mind and heart and touch with loving care that most tender, guarded, secret being hiding within impenetrable protective walls is my most passionate desire.

To let that being know that there are others like it—frightened, lonely creatures—in the midst of the hostilities of the surface world of sham people;

To form that tenuous thread of understanding between these secret beings;

To share life, this brief flash between two black eternities, with others of my ken . . . would seem to give it meaning.

I would be, or strive to be, a poet perhaps . . . a reacher . . . a dreamer . . . an artist painting thought pictures . . . a thought sculpturer using words as chisels . . . an architect of phrases.

But whatever, I must reach out and try to touch others.

—Howard Johnson, 1974

It remained necessary to prove which side you were on, to show your loyalty to the black masses, to strike out and name names.

—From Dreams of my Father - Barack Hussein Obama

A stitch in time, saves. He who hesitates, is. He who laughs, lasts. Great minds think. A penny saved is a penny. Actions speak louder. Idle hands are the Devil's.

—Howard Johnson, 1965

Success comes in CANS. Failure comes in CAN'TS.

—Dartnell

There are times when admitting defeat is the greatest victory.

—Howard Johnson, 1973

The best feeling in the world is to do a kindness in secret and have it discovered by accident.

—Unknown

Deceit can destroy only deceivers. No liar can perceive the purpose of him whose heart is free from treason to himself. Guile is a form of wisdom that an honorable man may have and honorably use, persuading deceivers to employ their ill will ignorantly in the service of him whom they aim to destroy.

—Howard Johnson, 1968

[Karl] Marx never did a day of work in his life, and never took the trouble to find out how a worker really feels when on the job. He naturally assumed that workers were a lesser breed of intellectuals.

—Eric Hoffer

Most men, it seems to me, do not care for nature and would sell their share in all her beauty for a given sum. Thank God men have not yet learned to fly so they can lay waste the sky as well as the earth.

—Henry David Thoreau

I have no yesterdays. Time took them away. I may not have tomorrow, but I have today.
—Pearl Yeadon McGinnis

Reality is that which, when you stop believing in it, doesn't go away.

—Philip K. Dick

To a liberal Democrat, socialist, or almost any intellectual, reality simply does not exist.
—Howard Johnson, 1998

    The past is that portion of time we carry in the storehouse of our memory and all before it. It includes memories, pleasant and unpleasant according to our heart.

    The future is that portion of time we carry in the dreams and wishes of our hearts. It is colored bright or dark according to our spirit.

    The now—today—that brief demarcation between past and future is where we act, live, dream, remember, plan, think, cry, laugh, and love. It is good or bad according to our motivating desire at that instant.

—Howard Johnson, 1965

You shall not go about spreading slander among your kinsmen; nor shall you stand by idly when your neighbor's life is at stake. I am the LORD.

—Leviticus Chapter 19:16 NIV

Life is a process. We are a process. The universe is a process.

—Anne Wilson Schaef

He who has no God is his own God and will live accordingly   *—Howard Johnson, 2007*

Ethics cannot be based upon our obligations toward [people], but they are complete and natural only when we feel this reverence for life and the desire to have compassion for and to help all creatures insofar as it is in our power. I think that this ethic will become more and more recognized because of its great naturalness and because it is the foundation of a true humanism toward which we must strive if our culture is to become truly ethical.
—*Albert Schweitzer*

Life is made up, not of great sacrifices or duties, but of little things, in which smiles and kindness and small obligations, given habitually, are what win and preserve the heart and secure comfort.
—*Sir Humphrey Davy, 1778-1829*

Dear Lord,
I want to say today I have not done a single bad thing. I have not been angry or nasty to anyone. I have not said an unkind word, acted selfishly, bragged, or cursed.
But in a few minutes, Lord, I am going to get out of bed, and from then on, I'll need all the help I can get.
—*Unknown*

During the next four years I will cut our federal deficit in half.
—*Barack Obama, 2008*

If, as Obama says, paying people not to work creates jobs, why not pay everyone not to work and there will be millions of jobs created. It must be true since our glorious leader says so.
—*Howard Johnson*

I can swear there ain't no Heaven, but I pray there ain't no hell.
—*A bit of religious philosophy from* **And When I Die**, *written by Laura Nyro and recorded by* **Blood, Sweat and Tears** *in 1969.*

A friendship founded on business is better than a business founded on friendship.
—*John D. Rockefeller (1874-1960)*

If

If you can keep your head when all about you
    Are losing theirs and blaming it on you;
If you can trust yourself when all men doubt you,
    And make allowance for their doubting too;
If you can wait and not be tired of waiting
    Or being lied about, don't deal in lies;
Or, being hated, don't give way to hating;
    And yet don't look too good, nor talk too wise;
If you can dream, and not make dreams your master;
    If you can think, and not make thoughts your aim;
If you can meet with triumph and disaster.
    And treat those two imposters just the same;
If you can bear to hear the truth you've spoken
    Twisted by knaves to make a trap for fools;
Or watch the things you gave your life to, broken,
    And stoop, and build them up with worn out tools;
If you can make one heap of all your winnings
    And risk it on one turn of pitch-and-toss,
And lose, and start again at your beginnings
    And never breathe a word about your loss;
If you can force your heart and nerve and sinew
    To serve your turn long after they are gone,
And so hold on when there is nothing in you
    Except the will which says to them: "Hold on!"
If you can walk with crowds and keep your virtues,
    Or walk with kings, nor lose the common touch;
If neither foes nor loving friends can hurt you,
    If all men count with you, but none too much;
If you can fill the unforgiving minute
    With sixty seconds worth of distance run,
Yours is the Earth and everything that's in it
    And, which is more, you'll be a man, my son!

—Rudyard Kipling, 1865–1936

It is not easy,
 To apologize,
  To begin over,
   To be unselfish,
    To take advice,
     To admit error,
      To face a sneer,
       To be charitable,
        To keep trying,
         To be considerate,
          To avoid mistakes,
           To endure success,
            To profit by mistakes,
             To forgive and forget,
              To think and then act,
               To keep out of a rut,
                To make the best of little,
                 To subdue an unruly temper,
                  To shoulder a deserved blame,
                   To recognize the silver lining,
                    But it always pays grand rewards!

—Ohio Educational Monthly, Author unknown

Grown-ups love figures. When you tell them that you have made a new friend, they never ask you any questions about essential matters. They never say to you, "What does his voice sound like? What games does he love best? Does he collect butterflies?" Instead, they demand: "How old is he? How many brothers has he? How much does he weigh? How much money does his father make?" Only from these figures do they think they have learned anything about him.

—Antoine de Saint-Exupéry, The Little Prince, 1943

It is better to have a permanent income than to be fascinating.

—Oscar Wilde (1854-1900)

The holiest of all holidays are those kept by ourselves in silence and apart; the secret anniversaries of the heart, when the full river of feeling overflows; the happy days unclouded to their close; the sudden joys that out of darkness start as flames from ashes; swift desires that dart like swallows, singing down each wind that blows!
—*Henry Wadsworth Longfellow, 1807–1882*

When things go wrong as they sometimes will,
When the road you're trudging seems all uphill,
When the funds are low and the debts are high
And you want to smile, but you have to sigh,
When care is pressing you down a bit,
Rest, if you must, but don't you quit.
Life is queer with its twists and turns,
As every one of us sometimes learns,
And many a failure turns about
When he might have won had he stuck it out;
Don't give up though the pace seems slow,
You may succeed with another blow.
Often the goal is nearer than,
It seems to a faint and faltering man,
Often the struggler has given up,
When he might have captured the victor's cup,
And he learned too late when the night slipped down,
How close he was to the golden crown.
Success is failure turned inside out,
The silver tint on the clouds of doubt,
And you never can tell how close you are,
It may be near when it seems so far;
So stick to the fight when you're hardest hit,
It's when things seem worst that you must not quit.
—*This has been credited to several writers,*
but the true author remains Unknown

We have no government armed with power capable of contending with human passions unbridled by morality and religion. Avarice, ambition, revenge or gallantry would break the strongest cords of our Constitution as a whale goes through a net. Our Constitution is designed only for a moral and religious people. It is wholly inadequate for any other.

—*John Adams*

Without violence nothing is ever accomplished in history.

—*Karl Marx*

Come with Me to Macedonia and Fight

Commanders should be counseled chiefly by persons of known talents; by those who have made the art of war their particular study, and whose knowledge is derived from experience; by those present at the scene of action, who see the enemy, who see the advantages that occasions offer, and who, like people embarked on the same ship, are sharers of the danger. If, therefore, anyone thinks himself qualified to give advice respecting the war which I am to conduct, let him not refuse assistance to the state . . . but come with me to Macedonia.

He shall be furnished with a ship, a horse, a tent; even his traveling charges shall be defrayed. But if he thinks this too much trouble and prefers the repose of the city life to the toils of war, let him on land not assume the office of the pilot.

The city in itself furnishes an abundance of topics for conversation; let it confine its passion for talking to its own precincts and rest assured that we shall pay no attention to any counsel, but as shall be framed within our camp.

—*Lucius Aemilius Paullus, Roman Consul, 168 BC*

A poet in a mirror is - a wind walker - a reacher for stars.
    The poet speaks - the mirror reflects - a few truly understand.

—*Howard Johnson, 1997*

The quickest way of ending a war is to lose it.

—*George Orwell*

The world has no room for cowards. We must all be ready somehow to toil, to suffer, to die. And yours is not less noble because no drum beats before you when you go out to your daily battlefields, and no crowds shout your coming when you return from your daily victory and defeat.

—*Robert Louis Stevenson*

Where is all the knowledge we lost with information?

—*T. S. Eliot*

The function of socialism is to raise suffering to a higher level.

—*Norman Mailer*

The sick in soul insist that it is humanity that is sick, and they are the surgeons to operate on it. They want to turn the world into a sickroom. And once they get humanity strapped to the operating table, they operate on it with an ax.

—*Eric Hoffer*

Finally, a word to describe 21st Century American government.
Ineptocracy (in-ep-toc'-ra-cy) - a system of government where the least capable to lead are elected by the least capable of producing; and, where the members of society least likely to sustain themselves or succeed, are rewarded with goods and services paid for by the confiscated wealth of a diminishing number of producers.

—*unknown*

Foreign aid might be defined as a transfer from poor people in rich countries to rich people in poor countries.

—*Douglas Casey*

A government policy to rob Peter to pay Paul can be assured of the support of Paul.

—*George Bernard Shaw*

We Americans engage each other in fierce inner political warfare, while our enemies stand on the sidelines urging on all sides, and gleefully watching our self destruction.

—*from the book,* **Energy, Convenient Solutions**,
Howard Johnson, 2010

Anything . . . that man can conceive of and believe in, can be accomplished.

—*Unknown*

Passionate hatred can give meaning and purpose to an empty life. Thus people haunted by the purposelessness of their lives try to find a new content not only by dedicating themselves to a holy cause but also by nursing a fanatical grievance. A mass movement offers them unlimited opportunities for both.

—*Eric Hoffer*

You see things; and you say, 'Why?'
But I dream things that never were; and I say, 'Why not?'

—George Bernard Shaw

In its original form (above), the quotation was said by the serpent in George Bernard Shaw's play *Back to Methuselah*.

Paraphrased, it was used by President Kennedy in his Speech to the Irish Parliament on June 28, 1963 as follows:

"Some men see things as they are and say 'why' - I dream things that never were and say 'why not.'"

Robert Kennedy made this quotation famous during his 1968 Presidential campaign. He paraphrased it as follows:

"Speaking as an Irishman [Shaw] summed up an approach to life: 'Other people see things and say: why - but I dream things that never were and say: why not.'"

—from Internet research

Even in our pursuit of happiness, there is some sadness and even evil. This is because we are less than perfect beings, with less than perfect minds and hearts, communicating in less than perfect means, in a less than perfect universe. The best we can do in this less than perfect world is just that, the best we can do.

—Howard Johnson, 2010

It is easier to talk about money -- and much easier to talk about sex -- than it is to talk about power. People who have it deny it; people who want it do not want to appear to hunger for it; and people who engage in its machinations do so secretly.

—Smiley Blanton

One valuable thing I learned about children is they belong to themselves, not to their parents. As parents, we are charged with guiding the infant into childhood, the child into a young adult, and the young adult into a full person. It's an awesome responsibility for which so many are ill trained. Parents who try to *possess* their children make a serious mistake and frequently drive them away. God loans us children for a short while, charging us with guiding them to independent adulthood and completely equal status. They are for us to teach, enjoy, love, and set free.

—Howard Johnson, 2010

I have learned only too well to understand—in part at least—the reason why I have felt my heart break and had to watch my pride burn in outward composure. Time and again, beneath a mask of composure and admirable manners, I have inwardly laughed at another's downfall. Yes, I know it. But I know no law that binds me to betray my grief when destiny permits another's malice to inflict a penalty I owe.
—*Talbot Mundy, from the log of Lord Tros of Samothrace*

I've learned in my lifetime so far that you can't help who you fall for and no matter how hard you try and how much it hurts you everyday that you just wanna be with them or just talk to them you never stop trying to make them happy by the little things you say or do because that's what makes your life worth going on for.
— *Unknown*

As you think, you travel; as you love, you attract. You are today where your thoughts have brought you; you will be tomorrow where your thoughts take you. You cannot escape the result of your thoughts, but you can endure and learn, and accept and be glad. You will realize the vision (not the idle wish) of your heart—be it base or beautiful, or a mixture of both—for you will always gravitate toward that which you secretly must love. Into your thoughts you will receive that which you earn—no more, no less. Whatever your present environment must be, you will fall, remain, or rise with your thoughts, your vision, your ideal. You will become as small as your controlling desire, as great as your dominant aspiration.
—*Howard Johnson, 1971*

Twenty years from now you will be more disappointed by the things that you didn't do than by the ones you did do. So throw off the bowlines. Sail away from the safe harbor. Catch the trade winds in your sails. Explore. Dream. Discover.
—*Mark Twain*

Hitherto I have found my real goal unattainable. But I persist, since the attainable is no more than a rung on the ladder of life on which a man may climb to grander view, though it will break beneath him if he lingers too long.
—*Talbot Mundy, from the log of Lord Tros of Samothrace*

Laughter and love are the handmaidens of joy. It's impossible to keep one without having the other. There can be no love without laughter and little joy without them both.
—*Chelton Chum in the novel, Blue Shift - Howard Johnson 2002*

At last we two are free! I of you, and you of me.
Love lying in its grave. Silence is all I crave.

—Unknown

If raising the minimum wage to $9 an hour is beneficial, why not raise it to $20, or even $50 and provide everyone a "living wage." Just think of all the workers who's income would grow and not be some paltry sum.

—Howard Johnson

The only way to get rid of a temptation is to yield to it.

—Oscar Wilde (1854-1900)

An honest man is always a child.

—Socrates

Most of us miss out on life's big prizes. The Pulitzer. The Nobel. Oscars. Tonys. Emmys. But we're all eligible for life's small pleasures. A pat on the back. A kiss behind the ear. A four-pound bass. A full moon. An empty parking space. A smile from a small child. A crackling fire. A great meal. A glorious sunset. Hot soup. Cold beer. Then there is the top prize, wonderful to experience. That prize is to do something nice for someone in complete and absolute secrecy and then have it discovered by accident.

—unknown

Somehow, we always get back to the basics. Right and wrong, good and evil, like beauty, are in the eye of the beholder (or doer). Their rules are not immutable. They are lifestyle—cultural, social, or religious creations. They depend entirely on one's own situation—whose side you are in, to what group you belong, or who eats whom. I am sure Genghis Khan, Hitler, and Saddam Hussein had and have quite different views from their victims of right and wrong.

Good and evil, right and wrong have very different meanings for a zebra than for a lion.

—Howard Johnson, May 8, 2001

Love me Sweet, with all thou art, feeling, thinking, seeing;
Love me in the lightest part, love me in full being.

Love me with thine open youth in its frank surrender;
With the vowing of thy mouth, with its silence tender.

Love me with thine azure eyes, made for earnest grantings;
Taking colour from the skies, can Heaven's truth be wanting?

Love me with their lids, that fall snow-like at first meeting;
Love me with thine heart, that all neighbours then see beating.

Love me with thine hand stretched out freely -- open-minded:
Love me with thy loitering foot, – hearing one behind it.

Love me with thy voice, that turns sudden faint above me; Love me with thy lush that burns when I murmur 'Love me!'

Love me with thy thinking soul, break it to love-sighing;
Love me with thy thoughts that roll on through living -- dying.

Love me in thy gorgeous airs, when the world has crowned thee;
Love me, kneeling at thy prayers, with the angels round thee.

Love me pure, as muses do, up the woodlands shady:
Love me gaily, fast and true, as a winsome lady.

Through all hopes that keep us brave, farther off or nigher,
Love me for the house and grave, and for something higher.

Thus, if thou wilt prove me, Dear, woman's love no fable,
I will love thee -- half a year – as a man is able.

— *Elizabeth Barrett Browning*

For the things we have to learn before we can do them, we learn by doing them.
—*Aristotle*

So, fall asleep love, loved by me... for I know love, I am loved by thee. Take away love and our earth is a tomb.

— *Robert Browning*

Two souls with but a single thought, two hearts that beat as one.
— *John Keats*

Aye . . . like a snowflake in flight
    between sky and ocean are we.
        Beauty for an instant . . . Never to be again.

—*Howard Johnson, 1973*

Without doubt the most famous love poem in English literature is this famous work.

> How do I love thee? Let me count the ways.
> I love thee to the depth and breadth and height
> My soul can reach, when feeling out of sight
> For the ends of Being and ideal Grace.
> I love thee to the level of every day's
> Most quiet need, by sun and candlelight.
> I love thee freely, as men strive for Right;
> I love thee purely, as they turn from Praise.
> I love with a passion put to use
> In my old griefs, and with my childhood's faith.
> I love thee with a love I seemed to lose
> With my lost saints, I love thee with the breath,
> Smiles, tears, of all my life! and, if God choose,
> I shall but love thee better after death.

– *Elizabeth Barrett Browning*

People are lonely because they build walls . . .
                             instead of bridges.

—*Joseph Forte Newton*

Ice-blue eyes - secret tears - pain hidden in the heart - bright laughter - running, running - broken child's world - stifled fears - steeled, hard-shell - soft love-warmth - sun and bright sky to black midnight - the now trapped - foiled understanding - tenuous dream-wish - listen, hear - being freedom - broken chains - fly to - reach - have - love - borrow - miss you
.

—*Howard Johnson, 1965*

Of all Life's difficulties I have found it hardest to compel myself to recognize and concede a woman's right to meet me on even terms. But it seems equally hard for a woman to understand my attitude. No more than all the priests, philosophers and poets do I know what love is. Unlike many of them, I am unwilling to pretend that I do know. Neither do I know what life is. But it seems to me that if love or life lack dignity, neither the one nor the other is worth the sacrifice of half a moment's thought.

—*Talbot Mundy* in Purple Pirate

True beauty is not in the eye but in the **heart** of the beholder!

—*Howard Johnson, 1968*

To be alone and without love is a waste of the heart.
To be with someone and without love is a waste of the soul.

—*How Chee Loo, 1863*

As dead flies give perfume a bad smell, so a little folly outweighs wisdom and honor. The heart of the wise inclines to the right, but the heart of the fool to the left. Even as he walks along the road, the fool lacks sense and shows everyone how stupid he is.

—*Ecclesiastes 10:1–3*

Words from a wise man's mouth are gracious, but a fool is consumed by his own lips. At the beginning his words are folly; at the end they are wicked madness—and the fool multiplies words.

—*Ecclesiastes 10:12–14*

"Let me be a free man. Free to travel. Free to stop. Free to work. Free to choose my own teachers. Free to follow the religion of my fathers. Free to think and talk and act for myself."

—*Chief Joseph, Nez Perce Indian Tribe*

The full use of your powers along lines of excellence.

—*definition of happiness by John F. Kennedy (1917-1963)*

I'm living so far beyond my income that we may almost be said to be living apart.

—*e e cummings (1894-1962)*

You can discover more about a person in an hour of play than in a year of conversation.

—*Plato*

I'll moider da bum.

—*Heavyweight boxer Tony Galento, when asked what he thought of William Shakespeare*

The only true wisdom is in knowing you know nothing.
— *Socrates*

I find that the harder I work, the more luck I seem to have.
— *Thomas Jefferson (1743-1826)*

Each problem that I solved became a rule which served afterwards to solve other problems.
— *Rene Descartes (1596-1650), Discours de la Methode*

In the End, we will remember not the words of our enemies, but the silence of our friends.
— *Martin Luther King Jr. (1929-1968)*

Whether you think that you can, or that you can't, you are usually right.
— *Henry Ford (1863-1947)*

Do, or do not. There is no 'try'.
— *Yoda ('The Empire Strikes Back')*

A hero is born among a hundred, a wise man is found among a thousand, but an accomplished one might not be found even among a hundred thousand men.
— *Plato*

To Do Is to Live

To do what you know you must when the time comes;
To be who you truly are in the face of ridicule;
To stand true and tall against strong opposition;
To give without hope of reward or repayment;
To believe for the sake of truth only . . .
And to love for the sake of love only . . .
. . . is to live!

— *Howard Johnson, 1963*

While visiting my daughter Kristen and her family with my two darling granddaughters, I found posted on a bulletin board some wise words from another grandfather from another time.

❖ ❖ ❖

An old Cherokee told his grandson, "My son, there is a battle between two wolves inside us all. One is evil: anger, jealousy, greed, resentment, inferiority, lies and ego. The other is good: joy, peace, love, hope, humility, kindness, empathy and truth."

The boy thought about it and asked: "Grandfather, which wolf wins?"

The old man quietly replied: "The one you feed."

The story starting on the next page is of my own grandfather and I, is in a similar vein. It was one of the most powerful life lessons I ever learned, even so, it took me many years to realize its value and importance and strive to live up to such an important lesson.

When a person, child or adult, exhibits anger, resentment or any other negative emotion they are feeding the evil wolf within them. Once expressed in words like, "I hate . . ." the individual must act out the meaning of their words in order to demonstrate their commitment to what they have said. This is true even when they realize they are wrong. As in a child's temper tantrum, anger feeds on its self and grows often doing injury and pain to the one who is angry. The evil wolf is being fed and all those bad feelings grow. How much better it is for everyone to stem that anger, forgive and forget, and let the good wolf win.

To My Dearly Beloved Grandchildren

Your kind of grandfather? Well, maybe! I wrote the previous message to your parents. Now it's your turn. Being a grandfather is a different experience and challenge. There is no choice, little direct responsibility, some commitment and yet, still more mixed blessings. Also, there is far more good than bad. For me, one of the hardest and most necessary things to do is to keep my mouth shut when I feel like spouting volumes, at least during the years before your maturity and independence. I hereby give notice, once you've left the nest and become fully adult, I no longer feel constrained and will freely share opinions about most everything. I urge you to pore through this book, or my other *Lakeside* books, *Memoirs from the Lakeside*, or *Words from the Lakeside*, in which this letter appears. There is far more of whom I am in these books than I could include in any letter.

Note especially those words which urge you to be independent, self-reliant, your own person, and to make your own way in life. Don't be a second edition of anyone; be who you are. The comfortable nest, once abandoned, can never be regained. Make your own nest where and when you choose. The silver umbilical cord must be discarded, or you and your parents will never share an adult relationship. I take great pleasure in my relationship with your parents. It is one independent human with another. I would only hope you will some day enjoy the same kind of unfettered relationship with your parents and, of course, with your grandfather.

My maternal grandfather, Granddad Dick (for Dickinson) was a marvelous companion and teacher for me when I was small. We spent many hours together, often fishing as described in one of the stories. One incident when I was quite young, six or seven probably, had a lasting and positive effect on my life. He and grandma were at our house for dinner, and mom was serving stewed turnips. When they were passed my way, I turned up my nose announcing, "I hate stewed turnips."

Granddad turned to me and said, "Howard, you should never say you hate anything. Say, 'I love stewed turnips,' and you'll be surprised how good they taste. It works Howard. Try it."

That won't work, I thought to myself, but since I held my granddad in such respect, and even awe, I decided to try it. I then bravely announced, "I love stewed turnips" while smiling at Granddad and at the same time helping myself to a large spoonful of turnips.

I could hardly believe it. They tasted delicious! I looked at Granddad and announced incredulously, "I do love stewed turnips."

"You see?" Granddads said smiling knowingly. "It does work, like I said it would."

To this day I love stewed turnips and a whole lot of other things I tried the same trick on. I have always believed my grandfather's dinner table lesson is the reason why I like so many foods to this day. There is almost nothing I am served I don't eat with relish—if it is well prepared.

This carried over onto all parts of my life, enforced by my natural tendency to go against the crowd—to resist peer pressure. Many boys repeat the mantra, *I hate school*, and then feel bound to prove it. I went against strong peer pressure saying repeatedly, "I love school."

Well, guess what? I always loved school and learning. There is no doubt in my mind I have used this principle to good effect on many other situations in my life. It is a powerful motivational force. I suggest you try it. No, don't try it, DO IT!

There are several memoirs in this book about Granddad Dick. You may gain some valuable insight from these stories from a man who taught me many worthwhile lessons about life. He was your great-great-granddad so you carry some of his genes.

To the youngest and the next generation, even though you don't know me or maybe never even met me, I will live on in the pages of this book as long as there are those who read it. Hopefully someone in the family will give you a copy. It's the legacy I am leaving for you. My hope is it will live on long after I'm gone.

—Howard Johnson 2009

The United States will be a socialist dictatorship by 2030. At this time those leftist activists will happily extol the joys of socialism as they are being carted off to the salt mines.

—Howard Johnson, 2008

With our progress we have destroyed our only weapon against tedium: that rare weakness we call imagination.

—Oriana Fallaci

Love Them and Let Them Be

Each of us must live within our own skins. No matter how much we want things for another, no how much we love and wish and cry and hope and pray, no matter how good our intent or noble our wishes, we are but bystanders to the pain, joy, sorrow, happiness, and love that another experiences—unless that other person lets us into their lives. So it is with children, parents, friends, and lovers. *Love them and let them be*, someone once said about children. So be it with others, even lovers. That decision lies fully within them as within us.

Sometimes it is extremely difficult to let go of that fierce loyalty one feels for one so dear we have lost. Sometimes I hurt terribly—tears flow, my heart aches, my mind reels! Barbara will always be who she was and still is to me. Yet I am moving on. I consider myself so fortunate to find out this new thing about myself—to love deeply and passionately once more and have it never touch negatively or diminish in any way what Barb and I had for the time we spent together. How wonderful that Daphne understands, and we can share moments of grief—cry together and then laugh together. I am indeed a fortunate human having met such women. God has been so kind to me in so many ways.

—*Howard Johnson, November 2006*

Every heart sings a song, incomplete, until another heart whispers back. Those who wish to sing always find a song. At the touch of a lover, everyone becomes a poet.

—*Plato*

A mathematician is a device for turning coffee into theorems.

—*Paul Erdos (1913-1996)*

But at my back I always hear Time's winged chariot hurrying near.

—*Andrew Marvell (1621-1678)*

Everybody pities the weak; jealousy you have to earn.

—*Arnold Schwarzenegger (1947-)*

Whenever I climb I am followed by a dog called 'Ego'.

—*Friedrich Nietzsche (1844-1900)*

Problems worthy of attack prove their worth by fighting back.
— *Paul Erdos (1913-1996)*

Never interrupt your enemy when he is making a mistake.
— *Napoleon Bonaparte (1769-1821)*

I have nothing to declare except my genius.
— *Oscar Wilde (1854-1900) upon arriving at U.S. customs 1882*

Human history becomes more and more a race between education and catastrophe.
— *H. G. Wells (1866-1946)*

The difference between 'involvement' and 'commitment' is like an eggs-and-ham breakfast: the chicken was 'involved' - the pig was 'committed'.
— *unknown*

He who has a 'why' to live, can bear with almost any 'how'.
— *Friedrich Nietzsche (1844-1900)*

Many wealthy people are little more than janitors of their possessions.
— *Frank Lloyd Wright (1868-1959)*

I'm all in favor of keeping dangerous weapons out of the hands of fools. Let's start with typewriters.
— *Frank Lloyd Wright (1868-1959)*

Some cause happiness wherever they go; others, whenever they go.
— *Oscar Wilde (1854-1900)*

Talent does what it can; genius does what it must.
— *Edward George Bulwer-Lytton (1803-1873)*

If you are going through hell, keep going.
— *Sir Winston Churchill (1874-1965)*

I don't know why we are here, but I'm pretty sure that it is not in order to enjoy ourselves.
— *Ludwig Wittgenstein (1889-1951)*

Give me a museum and I'll fill it.
—*Pablo Picasso (1881-1973)*

Don't stay in bed, unless you can make money in bed.
—*George Burns (1896-1996)*

There are no facts, only interpretations.
—*Friedrich Nietzsche (1844-1900)*

Nothing in the world is more dangerous than sincere ignorance and conscientious stupidity.
—*Martin Luther King Jr. (1929-1968)*

The use of COBOL cripples the mind; its teaching should, therefore, be regarded as a criminal offense.
—*Edsgar Dijkstra (1930-2002)*

C makes it easy to shoot yourself in the foot; C++ makes it harder, but when you do, it blows away your whole leg.
—*Bjarne Stroustrup*

Try to learn something about everything and everything about something.
—*Thomas Henry Huxley (1825-1895)*

He is one of those people who would be enormously improved by death.
—*H. H. Munro (Saki) (1870-1916)*

Individual rights are not subject to a public vote; a majority has no right to vote away the rights of a minority; the political function of rights is precisely to protect minorities from oppression by majorities (and the smallest minority on earth is the individual).
—*Ayn Rand*

Moral indignation is jealousy with a halo.
—*H. G. Wells (1866-1946)*

Glory is fleeting, but obscurity is forever.
—*Napoleon Bonaparte (1769-1821)*

Dream Thoughts

The mind drifts in and out of sleep on a Sunday morning.

It's early morning, those hours before my normal waking time. I'm in that delicious hazy state of drifting in and out of sleep moment by moment. During longer periods of being awake, I read about quantum physics and new thoughts about application of quantum effects on a cosmological scale. I read a paragraph or so, then sleep catches me for a few moments again, and the book slips from my grasp. Hazy thoughts and visions flow through my dream sleep of singularities, quantum fuzz, expanding universes, and celestial objects mixing with odd shapes and flashes of colored light—sensations of moving, falling, flying, and many indescribable ones. I see what I can't see, feel what I can't feel, and know what I can't know. The potent grasp of concepts of a universe, created by God and far too vast to see, fascinates me.

With powerful telescopes, astronomers can now see objects in every direction moving away from us at more than half the speed of light. Visions of moving to one most-distant part of the visual universe and looking back across that universe waft through my dream thoughts. I cannot see those known objects farthest from my new position since they are now receding faster than the speed of light relative to where I am. The light from these known objects will never reach me. I am moving away from them faster than the light they emit is traveling. As I am moving to my new location, those objects will *wink out"* when our relative departure reaches light speed.

Are we in a huge universe, forever limited to seeing only a tiny spherical part of an unimaginably vast space? This limit of and by the speed of light shuts us off from knowledge beyond that limiting sphere. In much the same way, time shuts us off from knowledge of the universe before the big bang, if that theory is correct. Does the force of gravity move at light speed, or is it instantaneous? We know that gravity *warps* light into a nearly parabolic path in much the same way as it *warps* the movement of objects. Perhaps light moves through the universe in a wavy, irregular path, accelerated and decelerated by the mass of objects it passes. Could it possibly move in a circular path if the universe is finite?

I imagine a roughly spherical shape for the universe. At the surface of this shape, all mass would be to one side of any point on the surface. The center of mass of this universe would be roughly at the geometric center. Could not light be warped by this center of mass so it could not escape from the universe? Could not the true speed of light be a factor of its distance from this center of mass? Maybe our measurement of light speed is a function of our own distance from this center of mass. Perhaps light passing through this center of mass is moving much faster than when it passes us. Likewise, light reaching the limit of the universe would slow and *fall* back in the same way one celestial body orbits another, controlled by the force of gravity. The limiting surface of the universe would act, in effect, as a kind of mirror, returning light and holding it within the gravitational grasp of the universe.

If this were the case, perhaps those faraway galaxies we see with our telescopes are viewed with light that has coursed many times through and around the universe. We may even be seeing our own galaxy millions or billions of years ago, possibly seeing it at numerous positions in the sky. How does one measure the effect or determine if such is the case? Our senses tell us that light moves in a perfectly straight line. We know this to be untrue as there are numerous objects we see in several different positions in space at the same time. The light has taken different paths to reach our observation, warped by what is called a gravitational lens. Could not this multiplication of apparent objects be occurring on a grand scale in the universe as a whole? Could not that galaxy we see far beyond Polaris actually be in the southern sky with its light taking an enormous circle through the universe before it reaches us? Our eyes and senses would straighten that irregular, roughly circular path, placing that galaxy in the northern sky rather than in its true position.

Our thoughts, even our dream thoughts, planted in a fertile field of the minds of men can grow new ideas and concepts which challenge the accepted. All great ideas flow into being in this manner. What prompts these dream thoughts? Is it God's hand at work or mere chance? Whether these thoughts from my mind are nonsense or a giant step forward remains to be seen. There are few mental seeds among the tons of chaff, few mental diamonds among acres of stones. These I share have been gleaned from many years of manipulations of dream thoughts prompted by input from many sources during my life. The future will decide whether they have substance or are mere feathers in the wind. Perhaps God's handiwork is showing. Perhaps this is another view of his creation. Perhaps the big bang was how he created our universe. We may never know, but the search for answers, the search for truth has to be man's greatest godly striving.

—*Howard Johnson, August 29, 1999*

There must always remain something that is antagonistic to good.

—*Plato*

An inconvenience is only an adventure wrongly considered; an adventure is an inconvenience rightly considered.

—*Gilbert Keith Chesterton (1874-1936)*

Be nice to people on your way up because you meet them on your way down.

—*Jimmy Durante*

Three o'clock is always too late or too early for anything you want to do.

—*Jean-Paul Sartre (1905-1980)*

Against stupidity, the gods themselves contend in vain.

—*Friedrich von Schiller (1759-1805)*

A doctor can bury his mistakes but an architect can only advise his clients to plant vines.

—*Frank Lloyd Wright (1868-1959)*

I have come to believe that the whole world is an enigma, a harmless enigma that is made terrible by our own mad attempt to interpret it as though it had an underlying truth.

—*Umberto Eco*

It is dangerous to be sincere unless you are also stupid.

—*George Bernard Shaw (1856-1950)*

If you haven't got anything nice to say about anybody, come sit next to me.

—*Alice Roosevelt Longworth (1884-1980)*

The significant problems we face cannot be solved at the same level of thinking we were at when we created them.

—*Albert Einstein (1879-1955)*

A man can't be too careful in the choice of his enemies.

—*Oscar Wilde (1854-1900)*

True Hell is when you realize you've made a stupid mistake and that someone else has to pay for your error.

—*Howard Johnson, 1966*

Forgive your enemies, but never forget their names.
—*John F. Kennedy (1917-1963)*

I shall not waste my days in trying to prolong them.
—*Ian L. Fleming (1908-1964)*

If you can count your money, you don't have a billion dollars.
—*J. Paul Getty (1892-1976)*

Facts are the enemy of truth.
—*Don Quixote - Man of La Mancha*

I begin by taking. I shall find scholars later to demonstrate my perfect right.
—*Frederick (II) the Great*

I am ready to meet my Maker. Whether my Maker is prepared for the great ordeal of meeting me is another matter.
—*Sir Winston Churchill (1874-1965)*

Maybe this world is another planet's Hell.
—*Aldous Huxley (1894-1963)*

Blessed is the man, who having nothing to say, abstains from giving wordy evidence of the fact.
—*George Elliott (1819-1880)*

Once you eliminate the impossible, whatever remains, no matter how improbable, must be the truth.
—*Sherlock Holmes (by Sir Arthur Conan Doyle, 1859-1930)*

Black holes are where God divided by zero.
—*Steven Wright*

All are lunatics, but he who can analyze his delusion is a philosopher.
—*Ambrose Bierce (1842-1914)*

Lord, protect me from my family and friends, my enemies I can handle myself.
—*unknown*

From the moment I picked your book up until I laid it down I was convulsed with laughter. Some day I intend reading it.
—*Groucho Marx (1895-1977)*

Basically, I no longer work for anything but the sensation I have while working.
—*Albert Giacometti (sculptor)*

There is more stupidity than hydrogen in the universe, and it has a longer shelf life.
—*Frank Zappa*

Many a man's reputation would not know his character if they met on the street.
—*Elbert Hubbard (1856-1915)*

It is far better to grasp the Universe as it really is than to persist in delusion, however satisfying and reassuring.
—*Carl Sagan (1934-1996)*

All truth passes through three stages. First, it is ridiculed. Second, it is violently opposed. Third, it is accepted as being self-evident.
—*Arthur Schopenhauer (1788-1860)*

Perfection is achieved, not when there is nothing more to add, but when there is nothing left to take away.
—*Antoine de Saint Exupery*

Life is pleasant. Death is peaceful. It's the transition that's troublesome.
—*Isaac Asimov*

If you want to make an apple pie from scratch, you must first create the universe.
—*Carl Sagan (1934-1996)*

There's a limit to how many times you can read how great you are and what an inspiration you are, but I'm not there yet.
—*Randy Pausch (1960-2008)*

A witty saying proves nothing.
—Voltaire (1694-1778)

The nice thing about being a celebrity is that if you bore people they think it's their fault.
—Henry Kissinger (1923-)

Education is a progressive discovery of our own ignorance.
—Will Durant

I have often regretted my speech, never my silence.
—Xenocrates (396-314 B.C.)

It was the experience of mystery -- even if mixed with fear -- that engendered religion.
—Albert Einstein (1879-1955)

If everything seems under control, you're just not going fast enough.
—Mario Andretti

I do not consider it an insult, but rather a compliment to be called an agnostic. I do not pretend to know where many ignorant men are sure -- that is all that agnosticism means.
—Clarence Darrow, Scopes trial, 1925.

There are people in the world so hungry, that God cannot appear to them except in the form of bread.
—Mahatma Gandhi (1869-1948)

Knowledge speaks, but wisdom listens.
—Jimi Hendrix

When you gaze long into the abyss, the abyss also gazes into you.
—Friedrich Nietzsche (1844-1900)

It is much more comfortable to be mad and know it, than to be sane and have one's doubts.
—G. B. Burgin

Everywhere I go I'm asked if I think the university stifles writers. My opinion is that they don't stifle enough of them.
—*Flannery O'Connor (1925-1964)*

I don't know anything about music. In my line you don't have to.
—*Elvis Presley (1935-1977)*

Dancing is silent poetry.
—*Simonides (556-468bc)*

If you can't get rid of the skeleton in your closet, you'd best teach it to dance.
—*George Bernard Shaw (1856-1950)*

No sane man will dance.
—*Cicero (106-43 B.C.)*

Music speaks what cannot be expressed, soothes the mind and gives it rest, heals the heart and makes it whole, flows from heaven to the soul.
—*Angela Monet*

Hell is a half-filled auditorium.
—*Robert Frost (1874-1963)*

Show me a sane man and I will cure him for you.
—*Carl Gustav Jung (1875-1961)*

If I were two-faced, would I be wearing this one?
—*Abraham Lincoln (1809-1865)*

The time is near at hand which must determine if Americans are to be free men or slaves.
—*George Washington*

The instinct of nearly all societies is to lock up anybody who is truly free. First, society begins by trying to beat you up. If this fails, they try to poison you. If this fails too, they finish by loading honors on your head.
—*Jean Cocteau (1889-1963)*

Everyone is a genius at least once a year; a real genius has his original ideas closer together.
—*Georg Lichtenberg (1742-1799)*

Success usually comes to those who are too busy to be looking for it
—*Henry David Thoreau (1817-1862)*

While we are postponing, life speeds by.
—*Seneca (3BC - 65AD)*

Where are we going, and why am I in this handbasket? —*Bumper Sticker*

God, please save me from your followers! —*Bumper Sticker*

First they ignore you, then they laugh at you, then they fight you, then you win.
—*Mahatma Gandhi (1869-1948)*

If thou of fortune be bereft, and in thy store there be but left,
Two loaves, sell one, and with the dole, buy Hyacinths to feed thy soul
—*Muslih-uddin Sadi*

Wit is educated insolence.
—*Aristotle (384-322 B.C.)*

My advice to you is get married: if you find a good wife you'll be happy; if not, you'll become a philosopher.
—*Socrates (470-399 B.C.)*

Advice is what we ask for when we already know the answer but wish we didn't
—*Erica Jong (1942-)*

I've learned that people will forget what you said, people will forget what you did, but people will never forget how you made them feel.
—*Maya Angelou (1928-)*

Egotist: a person more interested in himself than in me.
—*Ambrose Bierce (1842-1914)*

Show me a woman who doesn't feel guilty and I'll show you a man.

—*Erica Jong (1942-)*

A narcissist is someone better looking than you are.

—*Gore Vidal*

Wise men make proverbs, but fools repeat them.

—*Samuel Palmer (1805-80)*

Many a great proverb is read, shared with friends, and then forgotten. What a pity all that wisdom goes to waste.

—*Howard Johnson, 1998*

It has become appallingly obvious that our technology has exceeded our humanity.

—*Albert Einstein (1879-1955)*

The secret of success is to know something nobody else knows.

—*Aristotle Onassis (1906-1975)*

The power of accurate observation is frequently called cynicism by those who don't have it.

—*George Bernard Shaw (1856-1950)*

Sometimes when reading Goethe I have the paralyzing suspicion that he is trying to be funny.

—*Guy Davenport*

Most people would sooner die than think; in fact, they do so.

—*Bertrand Russell (1872-1970)*

Ignorance can be cured with education and experience. Stupidity furiously resists all efforts at correction or cure.

—*Howard Johnson, 1977*

We can easily forgive a child who is afraid of the dark; the real tragedy of life is when men are afraid of the light.

—*Plato*

When you have to kill a man, it costs nothing to be polite.
—*Sir Winston Churchill (1874-1965)*

Any man who is under 30, and is not a liberal, has no heart; and any man who is over 30, and is not a conservative, has no brains.
—*Sir Winston Churchill (1874-1965)*

The opposite of a correct statement is a false statement. The opposite of a profound truth may well be another profound truth.
—*Niels Bohr (1885-1962)*

We all agree that your theory is crazy, but is it crazy enough?
—*Niels Bohr (1885-1962)*

When I am working on a problem I never think about beauty. I only think about how to solve the problem. But when I have finished, if the solution is not beautiful, I know it is wrong.
—*Buckminster Fuller (1895-1983)*

In any contest between power and patience, bet on patience.
—*W.B. Prescott*

In science one tries to tell people, in such a way as to be understood by everyone, something that no one ever knew before. But in poetry, it's the exact opposite.
—*Paul Dirac (1902-1984)*

It is unbecoming for young men to utter maxims.
—*Aristotle (384-322 B.C.)*

Anyone who considers arithmetical methods of producing random digits is, of course, in a state of sin.
—*John von Neumann (1903-1957)*

Grove giveth and Gates taketh away   —*Bob Metcalfe (inventor of Ethernet) on the trend of hardware speedups not being able to keep up with software demands*

Reality is merely an illusion, albeit a very persistent one.
—*Albert Einstein (1879-1955)*

One of the symptoms of an approaching nervous breakdown is the belief that one's work is terribly important.

—*Bertrand Russell (1872-1970)*

A little inaccuracy sometimes saves a ton of explanation.

—*H. H. Munro (Saki) (1870-1916)*

There are two ways of constructing a software design; one way is to make it so simple that there are obviously no deficiencies, and the other way is to make it so complicated that there are no obvious deficiencies. The first method is far more difficult.

—*C. A. R. Hoare*

What do you take me for, an idiot?

—*General Charles de Gaulle (1890-1970), when a journalist asked him if he was happy*

I heard someone tried the monkeys-on-typewriters bit trying for the plays of William Shakespeare, but all they got was the collected works of Francis Bacon.

—*Bill Hirst*

I have voted hundreds of times, but only five times have I voted **for** a candidate. Every other time I had to choose the lesser of the evils presented on the ballot.

—*Howard Johnson, 1992*

Make everything as simple as possible, but not simpler.

—*Albert Einstein (1879-1955)*

Tragedy is when I cut my finger. Comedy is when you walk into an open sewer and die.

—*Mel Brooks*

Life may not be the party we hoped for, but while we are here, we might as well dance.

—*Rosie Giesie*

In the end, everything is a gag. —*Charlie Chaplin (1889-1977)*

The nice thing about egotists is that they don't talk about other people.
—Lucille S. Harper

You got to be careful if you don't know where you're going, because you might not get there.
—Yogi Berra

The only difference between me and a madman is that I'm not mad.
—Salvador Dali (1904-1989)

I love Mickey Mouse more than any woman I have ever known.
—Walt Disney (1901-1966)

He who hesitates is a damned fool.
—Mae West (1892-1980)

Good teaching is one-fourth preparation and three-fourths theater.
—Gail Godwin

University politics are vicious precisely because the stakes are so small.
—Henry Kissinger (1923-)

A clever man commits no minor blunders.
— Johann Wolfgang von *Goethe (1749-1832)*

Argue for your limitations, and sure enough they're yours.
—Richard Bach

To love oneself is the beginning of a lifelong romance
—Oscar Wilde (1854-1900)

Where your pleasure is, there is your treasure: where your treasure, there your heart; where your heart, there your happiness."
—Saint Augustine

Luck is the residue of design.
—Branch Rickey - former owner of the Brooklyn Dodger Baseball Team

Fill what's empty, empty what's full, and scratch where it itches.
> —*the Duchess of Windsor, when asked what is the secret of a long and happy life*

The graveyards are full of indispensable men.
> —*Charles de Gaulle (1890-1970)*

You can pretend to be serious; you can't pretend to be witty.
> —*Sacha Guitry (1885-1957)*

Behind every great fortune there is a crime.
> —*Honore de Balzac (1799-1850)*

If women didn't exist, all the money in the world would have no meaning.
> —*Aristotle Onassis (1906-1975)*

The object of war is not to die for your country but to make the other bastard die for his.
> —*General George Patton (1885-1945)*

I am not young enough to know everything.
> —*Oscar Wilde (1854-1900)*

Once is happenstance. Twice is coincidence. Three times is enemy action.
> —*Auric Goldfinger, in Goldfinger by Ian L. Fleming (1908-1964)*

Sometimes a scream is better than a thesis.
> —*Ralph Waldo Emerson (1803-1882)*

There is no sincerer love than the love of food.
> —*George Bernard Shaw (1856-1950)*

I don't even butter my bread; I consider that cooking.
> —*Katherine Cebrian*

I have an existential map; it has 'you are here' written all over it.
> —*Steven Wright*

Manuscript: something submitted in haste and returned at leisure.
—Oliver Herford (1863-1935)

Thank you for sending me a copy of your book - I'll waste no time reading it.
—Moses Hadas (1900-1966)

I have read your book and much like it.
—Moses Hadas (1900-1966)

The covers of this book are too far apart.
—Ambrose Bierce (1842-1914)

Few things are harder to put up with than a good example.
—Mark Twain (1835-1910)

Hell is other people.
—Jean-Paul Sartre (1905-1980)

Happiness is good health and a bad memory.
—Ingrid Bergman (1917-1982)

Now I am become death, the destroyer of worlds
—Robert J. Oppenheimer (1904-1967) (citing from the Bhagavad Gita, after witnessing the world's first nuclear explosion)

Friends may come and go, but enemies accumulate.
—Thomas Jones

You can get more with a kind word and a gun than you can with a kind word alone.
—Al Capone (1899-1947)

The gods too are fond of a joke.
—Aristotle (384-322 B.C.)

Distrust any enterprise that requires new clothes.
—Henry David Thoreau (1817-1862)

The difference between pornography and erotica is lighting.

—*Gloria Leonard*

It is time I stepped aside for a less experienced and less able man.

—*Professor Scott Elledge on his retirement from Cornell*

Every day I get up and look through the Forbes list of the richest people in America. If I'm not there, I go to work.

—*Robert Orben*

There are some experiences in life which should not be demanded twice from any man, and one of them is listening to the Brahms Requiem.

—*George Bernard Shaw (1856-1950)*

Attention to health is life's greatest hindrance.

—*Plato (427-347 B.C.)*

Plato was a bore.

—*Friedrich Nietzsche (1844-1900)*

Nietzsche was stupid and abnormal.

—*Leo Tolstoy (1828-1910)*

I'm not going to get into the ring with Tolstoy.

—*Ernest Hemingway (1899-1961)*

Hemingway was a jerk.

—*Harold Robbins*

Men are not disturbed by things, but by the view they take of things.

—*Epictetus (55-135 A.D.)*

What about things like bullets?

—*Herb Kimmel, Behavioralist, Professor of Psychology, upon hearing the above quote (1981)*

How can I lose to such an idiot?
—*A shout from chessmaster Aaron Nimzovich (1886-1935)*

And I looked, and behold a pale horse: and his name that sat on him was Death, and Hell followed with him.
—*Revelation 6:8*

Not only is there no God, but try finding a plumber on Sunday.
—*Woody Allen (1935-)*

I don't feel good.
—*The last words of Luther Burbank (1849-1926)*

I don't want to achieve immortality through my work; I want to achieve immortality through not dying.
—*Woody Allen (1935-)*

Nothing is wrong with California that a rise in the ocean level wouldn't cure.
—*Ross MacDonald (1915-1983)*

Men have become the tools of their tools.
—*Henry David Thoreau (1817-1862)*

I have never let my schooling interfere with my education.
—*Mark Twain (1835-1910)*

It is now possible for a flight attendant to get a pilot pregnant.
—*Richard J. Ferris, president of United Airlines*

The cynics are right nine times out of ten.
—*Henry Louis Mencken (1880-1956)*

I never miss a chance to have sex or appear on television.
—*Gore Vidal*

Men and nations behave wisely once they have exhausted all the other alternatives.
—*Abba Eban (1915-2002)*

Sanity is a madness put to good uses.

—George Santayana (1863-1952)

Morning	**Midnight**
Earth-lit moon,	White, black clouds
Pinking blue sky,	Black, black sky
Bird calls.	Gray-white moon
Volcano tips	Orion racing.
In gray cloud drips.	Gecko chirps,
Winding roads—misty	Waves on rocks,
Jeepneys, trikes,	splashing Invisible!
carabao carts, bikes.	Almost silence!
Children scampering,	Dreams.
Wet fields, shining	
Wind sound in Pines.	

—Howard Johnson, 1990

To sit alone with my conscience will be judgment enough for me.

—Charles William Stubbs

Imitation is the sincerest form of television.

—Fred Allen (1894-1956)

Always do right- this will gratify some and astonish the rest.

—Mark Twain (1835-1910)

In America, anybody can be president. That's one of the risks you take.

—Adlai Stevenson (1900-1965)

Copy from one, it's plagiarism; copy from two, it's research.

—Wilson Mizner (1876-1933)

When ideas fail, words come in very handy.

— Johann Wolfgang von Goethe (1749-1832)

The only truly stupid question is the one that is not asked.

—Howard Johnson, 1960

Why don't you write books people can read?
>—*Nora Joyce to her husband James (1882-1941)*

Some editors are failed writers, but so are most writers.
>—*T. S. Eliot (1888-1965)*

Criticism is prejudice made plausible.
>—*Henry Louis Mencken (1880-1956)*

It is better to be quotable than to be honest.
>—*Tom Stoppard*

Being on the tightrope is living; everything else is waiting.
>—*Karl Wallenda*

Opportunities multiply as they are seized.
>—*Sun Tzu*

A consensus means that everyone agrees to say collectively what no one believes individually.
>—*Abba Eban (1915-2002)*

A consensus means that everyone agrees to say collectively what no one believes individually.
>—*Abba Eban (1915-2002)*

A scholar who cherishes the love of comfort is not fit to be deemed a scholar.
>—*Lao-Tzu (570?-490? BC)*

The best way to predict the future is to invent it. —*Alan Kay*

Never mistake motion for action. —*Ernest Hemingway (1899-1961)*

I contend that we are both atheists. I just believe in one fewer god than you do. When you understand why you dismiss all the other possible gods, you will understand why I dismiss yours.
>—*Sir Stephen Henry Roberts (1901-1971)*

Hell is paved with good Samaritans.

—*William M. Holden*

Silence is argument carried out by other means.

—*Ernesto Che Guevara (1928-1967)*

The longer I live the more I see that I am never wrong about anything, and that all the pains that I have so humbly taken to verify my notions have only wasted my time.

—*George Bernard Shaw (1856-1950)*

Well done is better than well said.

—*Benjamin Franklin (1706-1790)*

The average person thinks he isn't.

—*Father Larry Lorenzoni*

Heav'n hath no rage like love to hatred turn'd, nor Hell a fury, like a woman scorn'd.

—*William Congreve (1670-1729)*

A husband is what is left of the lover after the nerve has been extracted.

—*Helen Rowland (1876-1950)*

Learning is what most adults will do for a living in the 21st century.

—*Lewis Perelman*

Dogma is the sacrifice of wisdom to consistency.   —*Lewis Perelman*

Sometimes it is not enough that we do our best; we must do what is required.

—*Sir Winston Churchill (1874-1965)*

The man who goes alone can start today; but he who travels with another must wait till that other is ready.

—*Henry David Thoreau (1817-1862)*

There is a country in Europe where multiple-choice tests are illegal.

—*Sigfried Hulzer*

Ask her to wait a moment - I am almost done.

—*Carl Friedrich Gauss (1777-1855), while working, when informed that his wife is dying*

A pessimist sees the difficulty in every opportunity; an optimist sees the opportunity in every difficulty.

—*Sir Winston Churchill (1874-1965)*

I think there is a world market for maybe five computers.

—*Thomas Watson (1874-1956), Chairman of IBM, 1943*

There are three unforgettable moments, good ones, bad ones, and embarrassing ones.

—*Howard Johnson, 1967*

Happiness is a warm puppy.

—*Charles M. Schulz*

I think it would be a good idea.

—*Mahatma Gandhi (1869-1948), when asked what he thought of Western civilization*

The fundamental cause of trouble in the world is that the stupid are cocksure while the intelligent are full of doubt.

—*Bertrand Russell (1872-1970)*

The only thing necessary for the triumph of evil is for good men to do nothing.

—*Edmund Burke (1729-1797)*

I'm not a member of any organized political party, I'm a Democrat!

—*Will Rogers (1879-1935)*

They who can give up essential liberty to obtain a little temporary safety deserve neither liberty nor safety.

—*Benjamin Franklin*

The U. S. Constitution doesn't guarantee happiness, only the pursuit of it. You have to catch up with it yourself.
—*Benjamin Franklin*

I never met a man I couldn't like.
—*Will Rogers (1879-1935)*

We don't like their sound, and guitar music is on the way out.
—*Decca Recording Co. rejecting the Beatles, 1962*

Everything that can be invented has been invented.
—*Charles H. Duell, Commissioner, U.S. Office of Patents, 1899*

Denial ain't just a river in Egypt.
—*Mark Twain (1835-1910)*

A pint of sweat saves a gallon of blood.
—*General George S. Patton (1885-1945)*

After I'm dead I'd rather have people ask why I have no monument than why I have one.
—*Cato the Elder (234-149 BC, AKA Marcus Porcius Cato)*

He can compress the most words into the smallest idea of any man I know.
—*Abraham Lincoln (1809-1865)*

If a Person Lives With Criticism
> He becomes one who condemns.

If a person lives with hostility
> He becomes one who fights.

If a person lives with ridicule
> He becomes shy.

If a person lives with shame
> He becomes one who feels guilty.

If a person lives with tolerance
> He becomes more patient.

If a person lives with praise
> He becomes one who appreciates

If a person lives with fairness
> He learns more of justice.

If a person lives with security
> He becomes one who has faith.

If a person lives with approval
> He becomes one who likes himself.

If a person lives with acceptance and friendship
> He becomes one who finds love in the world.

—*Paraphrased words of Dorothy Law Nolte by Howard Johnson, 2001*

Don't let it end like this. Tell them I said something.
—*last words of Pancho Villa (1877-1923)*

The right to swing my fist ends where the other man's nose begins.
—*Oliver Wendell Holmes (1841-1935)*

The concept is interesting and well-formed, but in order to earn better than a 'C', the idea must be feasible.

—A Yale University management professor in response to student Fred Smith's paper proposing reliable overnight delivery service - (Smith went on to found Federal Express Corp.)

All the gold which is under or upon the earth is not enough to give in exchange for virtue.

—Plato

The backbone of surprise is fusing speed with secrecy.

—Von Clausewitz (1780-1831)

Democracy does not guarantee equality of conditions - it only guarantees equality of opportunity.

—Irving Kristol

There is no reason anyone would want a computer in their home.

—Ken Olson, president and founder of Digital Equipment Corp., 1977

Who the hell wants to hear actors talk?

—H. M. Warner (1881-1958), founder of Warner Brothers, in 1927

If stupidity got us into this mess, then why can't it get us out?

—Will Rogers (1879-1935)

If you ignore the faith-based content of the Bible, it becomes a valuable history, a study of human nature, and an excellent guide to human behavior.

—Howard Johnson, 1967

For centuries, theologians have been explaining the unknowable in terms of the-not-worth-knowing.

—Henry Louis Mencken (1880-1956)

Pray, *verb.*: To ask that the laws of the universe be annulled on behalf of a single petitioner confessedly unworthy.

—Ambrose Bierce (1842-1914)

Fill the unforgiving minute with sixty seconds worth of distance run.

—Rudyard Kipling (1865-1936)

He would make a lovely corpse.

—Charles Dickens (1812-1870)

Every normal man must be tempted at times to spit upon his hands, hoist the black flag, and begin slitting throats.

—*Henry Louis Mencken (1880-1956)*

Now, now my good man, this is no time for making enemies.

—*Voltaire (1694-1778) on his deathbed in response to a priest asking that he renounce Satan.*

I've just learned about his illness. Let's hope it's nothing trivial.

—*Irvin S. Cobb*

I worship the quicksand he walks in.

—*Art Buchwald*

Wagner's music is better than it sounds.

—*Mark Twain (1835-1910)*

A poem is never finished, only abandoned.

—*Paul Valery (1871-1945)*

God gave men both a penis and a brain, but unfortunately not enough blood supply to run both at the same time.

—*Robin Williams, commenting on the Clinton/Lewinsky affair*

If you were plowing a field, which would you rather use? Two strong oxen or 1024 chickens?

—*Seymour Cray (1925-1996), father of supercomputing*

#3 pencils and quadrille pads.
  —*Seymoure Cray (1925-1996) when asked what CAD tools he used to design the Cray I supercomputer; he also recommended using the back side of the pages so that the grid lines were not so dominant.*

Interesting - I use a Mac to help me design the next Cray.

—*Seymoure Cray (1925-1996) when he was told that Apple Inc. had purchased a Cray supercomputer to help them design the next Mac.*

Woman was God's second mistake.
> —*Friedrich Nietzsche (1844-1900)*

Woman was God's second mistake.
> —*Friedrich Nietzsche (1844-1900)*

This isn't right, this isn't even wrong.
> —*Wolfgang Pauli (1900-1958), upon reading a young physicist's paper*

We are not retreating - we are advancing in another Direction.
> —*General Douglas MacArthur (1880-1964)*

There are only two tragedies in life: one is not getting what one wants, and the other is getting it.
> —*Oscar Wilde (1854-1900)*

There are only two ways to live your life. One is as though nothing is a miracle. The other is as though everything is a miracle.
> —*Albert Einstein (1879-1955)*

I am for those means which will give the greatest good to the greatest number.
> —*Abraham Lincoln*

It's not good enough that we do our best; sometimes we have to do what's required.
> —*Winston Churchill*

Opportunity is missed by most people because it is dressed in overalls and looks like work.
> —*Thomas Edison*

    I think he had one more vote than any other, and that placed him at the head of the committee. I had the next highest number, and that placed me the second. The committee met, discussed the subject, and then appointed Mr. Jefferson and me to make the draft, I suppose because we were the two first on the list.

    The subcommittee met. Jefferson proposed to me to make the draft. I said, 'I will not,' 'You should do it.' 'Oh! no.' 'Why will you not? You ought to do it.' 'I will not.' 'Why?' 'Reasons enough.' 'What can be your reasons?' 'Reason first, you are a Virginian, and a

Virginian ought to appear at the head of this business. Reason second, I am obnoxious, suspected, and unpopular. You are very much otherwise. Reason third, you can write ten times better than I can.' 'Well,' said Jefferson, 'if you are decided, I will do as well as I can.' 'Very well. When you have drawn it up, we will have a meeting.'
—*John Adams, 1822 letter to Timothy Pickering, published 1850.*

Get the facts first. You can distort them later.
—*Mark Twain*

The important thing is not to stop questioning.
—*Albert Einstein*

The greater the difficulty, the more glory in surmounting it. Skillful pilots gain their reputation from storms and tempests.
—*Epictetus (55-135 A.D.*

The most serious mistakes are not being made as a result of wrong answers. The truly dangerous thing is asking the wrong question.
—*Peter F. Drucker*

Dogs never bite me. Just humans.
—*Marilyn Monroe*

The greatest deterrent to Communism is an affluent, intelligent, and well-informed middle class.
—*Karl Marx*

The nearest way to glory is to strive to be what you wish to be thought to be.
—*Socrates*

The only man who makes no mistakes is the man who never does anything.
—*Theodore Roosevelt*

The pessimist sees difficulty in every opportunity. The optimist sees opportunity in every difficulty.
—*Winston Churchill*

Find something nice to say to everyone, each time you meet. Then say something nice about someone else to that person. If you do these two things consistently, your life will be pleasant, you will have many friends, and no one will ever find fault with you.
—*Howard Johnson, 1980*

Accuracy is the twin brother of honesty; inaccuracy, of dishonesty.
—*Charles Simmons*

People often say that motivation doesn't last. Well, neither does bathing-that's why we recommend it daily.
—*Zig Ziglar*

In England I would rather be a man, a horse, a dog, or a woman, in that order. In America I think the order would be reversed.
—*Bruce Gould*

Good advice is something a man gives when he is too old to set a bad example.
—*Francois de La Rochefoucauld*

This I beheld, or dreamed in a dream: - - There spread a cloud of dust along a plain; and underneath the cloud, or in it, raged a furious battle, and men yelled, and swords shocked upon swords and shields. A prince's banner wavered, then staggered backward, hemmed by foes.

A craven hung along the battles edge, and thought, "Had I a sword of keener steel—that blue blade that the king's son bears,—but this blunt thing!" he snapt and flung it far away and lowering, crept away and left the fray.

Then came the king's son, wounded, weak, and weaponless, and saw the broken sword hilt-burried in the dry and trodden sand, and ran and snatched it, and with banner lifted afresh he hewed his enemy down and saved a great cause that heroic day.
—*Edward Rowland Sill*

It is difficult to know what counts in the world. Most of us count credits, honor, dollars. But at the bulging center of mid-life, I am beginning to see that the things that really matter take place not in the boardrooms, but in the kitchens of the world.
—*Gary Allen Sledge*

"Do Unto Others as You Would Have Others Do Unto You."

The golden rule (Matthew 7:12 and Luke 6:31) is a direction for a way of life. It is simple and direct yet difficult for most to comprehend. It is a way for a person to act toward others, not something to be expected of them. One who applies the golden rule is a giver in the finest sense of the word and takes pleasure in the *giving*, with no thought of receiving anything whatsoever in return. Acceptance of the gift alone is the greatest kindness that a giver can receive.

Too often, we forget that others do not see the world as we do and are troubled that they do not seem to reciprocate our own imagined goodness. The golden rule has no component that says we should expect *anything* from another person. That is truly a function of *their* world, not ours. To expect any act from another is to burden ourselves with a potential disappointment and create tension in our interpersonal relationship with that individual. It is, in fact, the single most unkind action one can take toward another person.

Courtesy, consideration, friendship, affection, love—these are all giving things as *it is only in giving that we receive*. What we do receive is the pleasure of knowing what we have done and lies entirely within our own psyche with no external component. To expect or ask anything in return is to debase oneself and bring negative, displeasing specters into one's being.

"Judge not, that ye be not judged" (Matthew 7:1).

—Howard Johnson, 1978

The golden rule is of no use to you whatever unless you realize that it is your move!
—Dr. Frank Crane

If the only prayer you ever say in your whole life is "thank you," that would suffice
—Meister Eckhart

PANDORA'S SONG

Of wounds and sore defeat I made my battle stay;
Winged sandals for my feet I wove of my delay;
Of weariness and fear I made a shouting spear;
Of loss and doubt and dread and swift oncoming doom
I made a helmet for my head and a floating plume.
From the shutting mist of death and failure of the breath,
I made a battle horn to blow across the vales of overthrow.
O hearken where the echoes bring down the gray disasterous morn
Laughing and rallying!

—*Willliam Vaughn Moody*

Four things a man must learn to do
If he would make his record true;
To think without confusion clearly,
To love his fellow-men sincerely;
To act from honest motives purely;
To trust in God and Heaven securely.

—*Henry Van Dyke*

From the Hoosier poet:

When the frost is on the punkin and the fodder's in the shock,
And you hear the kyouck and gobble of the struttin' turkey-cock,
And the clackin' of the guineys, and the cluckin' of the hens,
And the rooster's hallylooyer as he tiptoes on the fence;
O, it's then's the times a feller is a-feelin' at his best,
With the risin' sun to greet him from a night of peaceful rest,
As he leaves the house, bareheaded, and goes to feed the stock,
When the frost is on the punkin and the fodder's in the shock.

They's something kindo' harty-like about the atmusfere
When the heat of summer's over and the coolin' fall is here --
Of course we miss the flowers, and the blossums on the trees,
And the mumble of the hummin'-birds and buzzin' of the bees;
But the air's so appetizin'; and the landscape through the haze
Of a crisp and sunny morning of the airly autumn days
Is a pictur' that no painter has the colorin' to mock --
When the frost is on the punkin and the fodder's in the shock.

The husky, rusty russel of the tossels of the corn,
And the raspin' of the tangled leaves, as golden as the morn;
The stubble in the furries -- kindo' lonesome-like, but still
A-preachin' sermons to us of the barns they growed to fill;
The strawsack in the medder, and the reaper in the shed;
The hosses in theyr stalls below -- the clover overhead! --
O, it sets my hart a-clickin' like the tickin' of a clock,
When the frost is on the punkin, and the fodder's in the shock!

Then your apples all is gethered, and the ones a feller keeps
Is poured around the celler-floor in red and yeller heaps;
And your cider-makin's over, and your wimmern-folks is through
With their mince and apple-butter, and theyr souse and sausage, too!
I don't know how to tell it -- but ef sich a thing could be
As the Angles wantin' boardin', and they'd call around on me --
I'd want to 'commodate 'em -- all the whole-indurin' flock --
When the frost is on the punkin and the fodder's in the shock!

—"The Hoosier Poet" James Whitcomb Riley (1849-1916)

The following poem, *Too Soon Old*, was written by Dave Griffith of Fort Worth, Texas. Griffith told **TruthOrFiction.com** he wrote the poem more than 20 years ago and meant for it to be simple, and to the point, from youth through old age in his own personal life, high school football, Marines, marriage, the ravages of his own disabilities.

Someone took the poem from his site, created a false story about it, and started it circulating on the Internet. None of this took away any of the value of the poem.

Griffith is the author of more than 500 poems, now posted on his personal website.

http://www.palletmastersworkshop.com/

I contacted him and received permission to use his poem in this book.

Too Soon Old - (Crabby Old Man)

What do you see nurses? . . . . . What do you see?
What are you thinking . . . . . when you're looking at me?
A crabby old man . . . . . not very wise,
Uncertain of habit . . . . . with faraway eyes?

Who dribbles his food . . . . . and makes no reply
When you say in a loud voice . . . . . "I do wish you'd try!"
Who seems not to notice . . . . . the things that you do,
And forever is losing . . . . . a sock or shoe.

Who, resisting or not . . . . . lets you do as you will,
With bathing and feeding . . . . . the long day to fill.
Is that what you're thinking? . . . . . Is that what you see?
Then open your eyes, nurse . . . . . you're not looking at me.

I'll tell you who I am . . . . . as I sit here so still,
As I do at your bidding, ... as I eat at your will.
I'm a small child of ten . . . . . with a father and mother,
Brothers and sisters . . . . . who love one another.

A young boy of sixteen . . . . . with wings on his feet.
Dreaming that soon now . . . . . a lover he'll meet.
A groom soon at twenty . . . . . my heart gives a leap.
Remembering, the vows . . . . . that I promised to keep.

At twenty-five, now . . . . . I have young of my own
Who need me to guide . . . . . and a secure happy home.
A man of thirty . . . . . my young now grown fast,
Bound to each other . . . . . with ties that should last.

At forty, my young sons . . . . . have grown and are gone,
But my woman's beside me . . . . . to see I don't mourn.
At fifty, once more . . . . . babies play 'round my knee,
Again, we know children . . . . . my loved one and me.

Dark days are upon me . . . . . my wife is now dead.
I look at the future . . . . . shudder with dread.
For my young are all rearing . . . . . young of their own,
And I think of the years . . . . . and the love that I've known.

I'm now an old man . . . . . and nature is cruel.
Tis jest to make old age . . . . . look like a fool.
The body, it crumbles . . . . . grace and vigor, depart.
There is now a stone . . . . . where I once had a heart.

But inside this old carcass . . . . . a young guy still dwells,
And now and again . . . . . my battered heart swells.
I remember the joys . . . . . I remember the pain,
And I'm loving and living . . . . . life over again.

I think of the years, all too few . . . . . gone too fast,
And accept the stark fact . . . . . that nothing can last.
So open your eyes, people . . . . . open and see.
Not a crabby old man . . . Look closer . . . see ME!!

— ©*David L. Griffith - 1990*

> Writers love to write.
> Writers live to write.
> Writers love to live.
> Writers live to love.
>   - - - - - Sometimes we cry.

—Howard Johnson - 2008

ACKNOWLEDGEMENTS

The quotes of other writers are acknowledged right below their quote. There may be a few erroneous credits even though I took great pains to properly identify the originator. I found a number of quotes attributed incorrectly by my sources. Mark Twain seemed to be the one whose words were most often attributed to later writers. Plato was another with about half the number of Mark Twain.

A large number of the short quotes came from a single source on the Internet. That source was a collection made by Dr. Gabriel Robins, Professor of Computer Science, Department of Computer Science, School of Engineering and Applied Science, University of Virginia. The web site is **http://www.cs.virginia.edu/~robins/**

www.ingramcontent.com/pod-product-compliance
Lightning Source LLC
Chambersburg PA
CBHW081456040426
42446CB00016B/3271